FATHER, FORGIVE MY FATHER

BY

SANDRA G. LEE

authorHOUSE™

1663 LIBERTY DRIVE, SUITE 200
BLOOMINGTON, INDIANA 47403
(800) 839-8640
WWW.AUTHORHOUSE.COM

First published by AuthorHouse 10/03/05

ISBN: 1-4208-6648-6 (e)
ISBN: 1-4208-6650-8 (sc)

Printed in the United States of America
Bloomington, Indiana

This book is printed on acid-free paper.

Table of Contents

FOREWARD

By Dana Gamble, Father's Hand Ministries
Roseburg, OR

I dare you to read this book. Sandy's subject matter is not light reading and makes many people uncomfortable. It is not entertaining, nor is it the center of conversations at casual dinner parties. To be hearing about abuse and incest happening in our country, state, city or right next door seems to be a subject we all want to avoid. As you are walking downtown, you are bumping into countless victims and their abusers without even seeing them. You don't even realize that they are there because this is a crime done in secret. It is too private, too hidden, and too close.

Sandy is writing this book because she needs to see people freed from a secret that has been kept quiet for too long. Many have closed their eyes to the reality of incest because it is just too ugly. I dare you to read this book and not come to realize your lack of knowledge about this epidemic that is happening all over; to our children.

After years of being separated, we two friends have been reunited. She was always a Christian witness when I knew her, but the tragedies of her life seemed to keep her from having victory. Her Christianity interested me, but I did not want her religion. I was a drug selling, alcohol guzzling piece of work when she knew me so many years ago. Her daughter babysat for us, and I was the 4-H leader for the local horse club her daughter attended. I was a liar and a cheat, but I kept that a secret along with all the rest of my pain. What did these two ladies from totally different lifestyles have in common? I was a victim of incest also, and was doing everything I could to find a reason to get up each day without wanting to end my life. She didn't know all this. She just saw a lost soul and reached out to me with great kindness and love. She knew something that I didn't. I was suffering from the after effects of years of sexual abuse from someone in my family. She had to point it out to me; I had no idea. Sandy and I went to group therapy together and we found out that what we had endured has happened to many young girls in similar situations. She was a true friend to me and helped me along my way as she was leaning on Jesus to get her through. Many years later I became a Christian, but had no way to tell her what she had done in my life. Getting back in touch with her has completed a chapter in my life.

After 25 years Sandy and I have found that our friendship has endured the test of time. When I knew her back then she was talking about writing this book and I encouraged her to follow through with it. I knew that it was in her heart, and hoped that by writing it she would find her healing and guide others to theirs.

Go ahead and read this book. You might be a victim. You may be an abuser. All it could ever do is change your point of view, or your life, or your reason to live. Go ahead and walk in Sandy's shoes, and see what she has found that has made it possible for her to live in peace. You may discover something along the way that will move you. I dare you.

PREFACE-

"Why did you write the book?" people who have not walked with me in the experience have asked me; "Why would you put yourself through all of that all over again?" I tell them that first (and most important) was a promise that I *had* to fulfill; I will share much more on that later. However, my other motivation was actually four fold: 1) to inform the general public of an increasingly serious social problem that is of epidemic proportion; 2) to help the victims of incest and sexual child abuse to better cope with and handle their problems through Christian principles and methods, at the same time assuring them that they are not alone in their struggles, 3) to bring the offenders of child abuse to a realization of what they are doing, why they are doing it, and ultimately help them to seek help and to realize there is a loving God who forgives this transgression, and finally, 4) to lead the victim through the steps to total healing through forgiveness.

Most of the information in this book has been formulated as a result of my own personal experience as a victim of incest over fifteen years, as well as one who has participated in group therapy sessions. I have seen the hurt, confusion and destruction of others who have been maimed by this atrocity. As a youth leader in churches for many years, I came in contact with too many young people who cried out for recognition. One way or another, they would grab our attention in their unconscious search to find someone (*anyone*) who would care, and would actually act to help them. I could not in all good consciousness ignore what I knew my heart and my God wanted me to do with this experience and knowledge. Therefore, I recommend the reading of this book above other self-help books on the same subject, because I firmly believe these revelations and principles of healing were orchestrated and inspired by a power much higher than myself or anyone else. These principles **work** if only you apply them.

I had felt the promptings early on to write about this experience when I was a young girl struggling through it. This poem that I found stuck in the pages of my youthful diary (that I wrote when I was approximately 12 years old) is the guiding force behind my determination to follow through and complete my promise to God. In reading it even today, I can feel all over again, how it felt to be hurting so much, to be crying out to God for his help and guidance. In my loneliness and pain I wrote:

"FATHER, FORGIVE MY FATHER"

Father, forgive my father,

He's done what he hadn't aught to.

He treats me like his mistress,

But I'm just his little daughter!

When things get really bad,

And all I feel is mad,

I'm so thankful you're my friend, Lord,

You're all that makes me glad.

Someday when I'm grown up,

I'll share You in a book,

About these sad, sad days,

And make others take a look.

Till then, Lord, be my guide;

Help me to not run and hide.

I'll share these sorrows only with You,

'Cause You're always by my side.

The information in this book has also been compiled through researching this sensitive subject and through sharing and interacting with other victims. I pray that it will help you personally and others your life touches, and, trust you will in turn pass this book on to them. I challenge you to do as I did, to share your hurts, give them to God, and, walking through the Biblical steps, let him touch you with his merciful healing power. Let Him touch you and heal those ugly scars so that you, too, can have victory.

INTRODUCTION
DO YOU REALLY KNOW WHAT'S HAPPENING NEXT DOOR?
DO YOU CARE?

Through my personal experience, and knowledge of the problems of sexual child abuse, and a complete faith in God and His ultimate plan for each of us, I present this book from a Christian viewpoint. My fervent prayer is that it will be a comfort and help to the countless victims, the offenders, and the families of both who are tormented and affected by this heinous crime in our society. I believe that people of all ethnic and social backgrounds will be interested in and benefit from reading a book of this nature, while many will relate to it on a personal level.

During my research for this project I came across many articles and a few books written by other victims. However, when the book was first birthed in my mind some forty plus years ago, there were not many written with a Christian point of view, or that gave testimony to the fact that the Lord was their salvation through it all. It astounded me at that time that there hadn't been more Christian literature written on the subject of sexual child abuse.

I know now that as a result of my faith in God this kind of abuse was *somewhat* easier for me than others I have read about (because I could always talk to Jesus about it while I was growing up). But, aside from that, I now feel a tremendous desire to come forward with "my story". I want to let people know what it was like to experience the seemingly never ending years of constant abuse, the loneliness of betrayal, and how I managed to get through it all.

Since I firmly believe that God has inspired me to write this book, I have to believe that He has in his hand the perfect timing for it to unfold. Again, He is bringing about something good from something bad. At the very earliest promptings from the Lord to write a book, I had very negative thoughts: "Who am I to write a book? I'm not a writer." I put it off and put it off, and each time the Lord would do something that would "bump" me again. So, I began to really pray hard about it, and then the answer finally came. He put such a rush of words into my head that I couldn't write them down fast enough (that was in the days before computers were second nature). I began to pray for a typewriter, and that Christmas I was pleasantly surprised when the Lord gave me one. Still, the enemy has many ways of robbing and stifling us in his search to seek out and devour those who he might, and he constantly put up roadblocks; thus, the many years of needless delay in completing a book to God's glory. Even in the final stages of writing, the enemy would try to steal it before it is finished. I have recently met with much opposition from my family who are fearful that people will "know who we are", and that we will be subjected to ridicule and judgment as a result of this writing. I state emphatically at this time that I do not now, nor have I ever, meant to harm my family through this revelation. Quite the contrary: I feel that the very fact that we are still "family", and a close one at that, testifies to the fact that we have gone through much healing, and are very much in tact as a fully functional family. Oh, sure, if I'm to be completely honest, I have to admit that we all have our <u>very</u> human side, the little quirks and remnants of our past that make us very individualistic. However, we all have a close, unconditional love for each other, and have chosen to accept and love one another for who we have become; for who we are now. That is how we have learned to function as "family".

However, I am somewhat ashamed, but not daunted, by the fact that it took me so long to grow-up to enough spiritual and emotional stability to complete the task of writing this book. I have dabbled at writing it in excess of three decades, and have only felt truly motivated to get it published in the past several years. A lot of that is due to the fact that I am retired now and have more time to apply to the project. However, I also know that a lot of the delay was because my experience left me for years in a state of disrepair, and I made wrong choices by always feeling that I had to "fix" everyone. But those years, however painful, have been for God's purpose, and not my own, and I have allowed Him to use me as His instrument in writing this work. Praise our wonderful, understanding, healing God! And, every once in awhile He gives me new affirmations that I am to press on. This morning as I watched "The Hour of Power" on the television, the guest speaker was Corretta Scott King, the widow of Dr. Martin Luther King, Jr. In her wonderful wisdom she said something that I knew, but that I needed to hear right now. "If God calls you to do something, He will equip you to do it." He will give you everything you need to accomplish the task. So I carry on and trust that He will.

Believing as I do that the Lord has led me to write this book, I feel sure that it will be beneficial information to many: not only to the abused, but also to the offenders, families of both, pastors, teachers, teens and parents. I believe it affects all of society when an offense affects one out of four young girls, and at least one out of seven boys before they reach the age of 18. In other words, in all reality, it should be of interest to everyone. If they don't already know, the public *must* be made aware of an epidemic that has spread like wildfire across our country. The abused must realize that they can come out of the woodwork, get the help they need, and learn to exercise Godly forgiveness. I believe the future of the family unit and that of society depends on bringing to the surface this intimate subject that all too long has been kept buried. Lord, with your guidance, I share "My Story" to your everlasting glory.

CHAPTER ONE

"MY STORY"
THE EARLY YEARS

As I lay in the still, calm darkness of my room that night I could feel the pounding of my heart and the tensing of my young, shuddering body. As on many such nights, each time this horrible thing repeated itself, I felt as if I'd never be able to relax my muscles or calm my heart again. The silence in the house seemed to deafen my ears as I waited in the stone still quietness, dreading what I knew was inevitable. My father had told me before bed that night something he had said many times before, to "be ready". That meant that when my mother and brother were finally asleep, he would come to my room. Did it matter to him that I lay here eaten away by this sickening fear that consumed my body? Did it matter that I needed my rest on a school night? (He was always after me to get better grades and to "live up to my potential"). But sleep wouldn't come easily tonight, either before or after he came. As I lay there waiting in the dark, I secretly wished that he would die before he got to me again. I had told him over and over how much I hated this constant thing that he forced upon me; I thought at the time that it was his all- consuming lust that made him completely unreasonable. Then I reasoned in later years that it was attention, acceptance and complete admiration

1

that he actually sought. Men who are unsure of themselves often seek these relationships in search of total acceptance. Little did I know at that time that a firm *"NO"* might have discouraged him, as this would have been a form of rejection that he probably would have wanted to avoid. I have since learned through counseling and studying human psychology that it was "**complete control**" that he actually sought. It just seemed to me at the time that he was completely oblivious to the fact that I hated him and what he was doing to me. I'm sure he kidded himself with the sick justification that I "liked it", and that probably made it okay for him and kept him from feeling guilty. I remember as a child asking him many times, "How can you do this Daddy, to your own flesh and blood?" Then he'd say, "I guess I just love you too much; I want to love you every way possible." I don't believe to this day that he ever knew the real meaning of love. I found this later, and I like to think of love in the terms of this poem written by Helen Steiner Rice:

THE MAGIC OF LOVE

Love is like magic
And it always will be,
For love still remains
Life's sweet mystery!

Love works in ways
That are wondrous and strange
And there's nothin' in life
That love cannot change!

Love can transform
The most commonplace
Into beauty and splendor
And sweetness and grace!

Love is **unselfish,**
Understanding and **kind,**
For it sees with its heart
And not with its mind!

Love is the answer
That everyone seeks—
Love is the language
That every heart speaks.

Love can't be **bought**
It is **priceless** and **free.**
Love like pure magic
Is a sweet mystery!

By Helen Steiner Rice

Used with permission of The Helen Steiner Rice ™ Foundation, Cincinnati, Ohio www.helensteinerrice.com. Copyright 1970 The

Sandra G. Lee

Based on those reflections and what I believe love really is, I can't go along with what he said, or believe that his motives were guided by his "love" for me. For one thing: Love is <u>unselfish</u>. He certainly was not being unselfish in the needless anxiety he caused his daughter, not to mention the lost hours of sleep she suffered, the guilt feelings of having betrayed her own mother while she slept, and the constant feelings of hate she felt toward her father. After many years I realized that I also had a deep resentment for my younger brother, too, as he slept in the next room and never came to my aid. Years later after we became adults, I discussed these feelings with him; he told me he knew that "something" was not quite right and that I was somehow suffering. He said, "Many times I wanted to go in and kill him, and many times I did, in my mind and heart." So, unbeknownst to me at the time, my brother was living a torment, too. He also was held in the bondage of fear, as Dad had unleashed his unreasonable wrath on him for years as he verbally and physically abused him. The last paragraph of the poem states very well, I believe, that "love can't be bought, it is priceless and free. He certainly made me pay for every bit of "love" I ever received from him.

Those nights of my childhood were terrible beyond words. I

4

still get butterflies in my stomach just thinking about them. Like I said, late at night after my brother in the next room, and my mother across the hall were asleep, he'd come to my room. Many times I remember pretending to be asleep and hoping that he couldn't hear the thump, thump, thump of my heart. Sometimes it worked and he'd leave, but most of the time it was impossible and he'd talk or threaten to make noise if I didn't respond, so that the others would wake up. So, then I'd let him do what he wanted with me, to keep him quiet, and it would be over more quickly. I guess I had more fear of a confrontation and violence between my parents than I had of his abuse. His "thing" or objective was trying to bring me to an orgasm; more **control** (but at that time I just thought, that's how he got his kicks). I suppose I can be grateful that he never tried to have actual intercourse with me, just fondled and penetrated with his fingers, so that I was sore most of the time. During these times I learned how to become real adept at having a quick orgasm so that he'd leave me alone sooner. He got wise to that, though, and before long began to play games with me. He'd say (and I still hate thinking of the sick sound of these words), "Don't go off too soon now; I want to play awhile and make it last." I reasoned that I would get even with him, and got so that I wouldn't do him the honor of having an orgasm at all. THAT really made him furious and I imagine was a real blow to his ego and masculinity. Probably most discouraging to him of all was that he lost some control over me. I often wonder why that alone didn't make him stop; but it didn't. As a result of his turning me on and off like a light switch, I feel as if he made a "sexual yo-yo" out of me. I firmly believe that is the reason I've had problems over the years in reaching total sexual fulfillment. Even though now, in my sunset years, I have a loving husband who is gentle and thoughtful of my needs, there is often a mental block there that makes fulfillment nearly impossible.

You know----in all my young years I never remember ever being able to just climb up on my Daddy's lap and have him love me; really love me, as every little girl wants and needs to be loved by her father. I remember well being so envious and jealous of my younger brother (even though I realized in later years that he had endured verbal and physical abuse from our father). In the early mornings he would get up and run cheerfully into the living room and hop up into my mother's warm lap. He'd always say, "Let's go love in the big blue chair." That was their time together, to chat and just be close, and I yearned for that relationship with my father, too. Oh, fathers who read this, love your little girls and your sons as God loves them, unconditionally and unselfishly, and not for what you can gain. Then perhaps, just maybe, your child will be able to feel real love from her father. Hopefully, she will not go from childhood to womanhood so starved for affection that she seeks a father image when she marries. I say this because, unconsciously, that is exactly what I did. My first husband was a man considerably older than I was. I feel this happened because, first of all, I was seeking an escape from home, and secondly, because I was unconsciously seeking someone as a father image. Although we were in love and had two beautiful children together, a son and a daughter 3 years apart, because of factors I will expand upon later, the marriage only lasted seven and a half years.

As a young girl, although tempted constantly to run away, I never left home for fear my father would take out his anger and revenge on my mother or brother. I had seen him react violently with both of them throughout the years, and firmly believed that they would be in danger if I were to leave home. An incident that happened when I was in junior high school reinforced this belief. I had read in the paper one evening that one of my girlfriends had reported her father for incest, and they had put him in prison. That gave me an idea! I could hold that over Dad's head and he would have to stop. That night when Dad came home from work, I waited until we were alone in the living room and Dad had set down in his chair. I tossed the newspaper in his lap and told him to read the article I pointed out to him. He read it, and looked up with a questioning look on his face. I felt really confident at that moment and told Dad, "If you don't stop bothering me, that's what I'm going to do to you!" He immediately jumped up, grabbed me forcefully by the arm, squeezing it till it hurt. Then he said very firmly with that hateful look in his eyes, "If you do, I'll start with you, and I'll kill the whole family." That was threat number two that threatened to destroy my family, because the first threat, much more subtle, had actually come years earlier when I was but three years old. My baby brother had just been born and home from the hospital a few days when this incident happened. Dad had first sexually abused me (two weeks before my third birthday) when Mom was in the hospital having my brother. One day soon after they were home I came into the kitchen while she was bathing my baby brother in the kitchen sink. I was still very upset about what had happened while she was gone, and, looking up at her said, "Mommy, when you were gone to the hospital, Daddy tickled my potty, and I didn't like it." She looked shocked, as if someone had stabbed her with a knife, but looked angry at the same time. She said with grimace on her face, "Your father wouldn't do such a thing, and if he did, I'd probably kill him." I left the kitchen in stark still shock, trying to imagine the terrible thing she had just threatened. Years later when I went through group counseling, they explained that those were the threats that held me in a bondage of fear, and kept me silent all those years. I was so afraid that if I said anything to anyone, something bad would happen, my family would be split apart or my parents would kill each other. Then years later I can remember wishing they would divorce or that Dad would die or leave us. But when that didn't happen, I always just kept wishing and waiting for the day when I would be old enough to leave home. That day could not come soon enough!

<u>CHAPTER TWO</u>

<u>TIME TO LEAVE HOME AT LAST</u>

Although the years passed slowly, the day to leave home finally came. Two days after my high school graduation in 1961 found me 1200 miles away, by car, working in a nationally famous summer resort. We had been able to make arrangements the summer before when our family was there on vacation. My grandmother knew the owners and put in a good word for me, and that's all it took, I was on my way...at last! Mother and I drove out there together and had a great time away from my Dad; it was a very relaxing trip. Mom stayed for a while in a motel three miles from the resort, making sure that I was settled into my dorm and the job was going smoothly, and then she was gone back home. I felt totally and completely FREE.

Those summer months were fantastic!! There was time to try my wings at working on my own, and even more important, a time to breathe freely for the first time in my life. Oh, sweet freedom, I was at last away from my father. I missed my home, family and friends, but it was more than worth it. I even had a couple of nice boyfriends that summer, but, of course, avoided any sexual involvements. Boys were more like big brothers that summer and I enjoyed the relationships. I stayed as long as I could, working past the summer months, signing up to work through October when most of the other kids went back to college (I would extend it as long as I could). But, all too soon the tourist season would be over, and I would eventually have to return home. Dad was already writing, saying how anxious he and Mom were for my return. I <u>knew</u> what "anxious" meant. It was cold that month, and the first snowfalls fell in the mountains surrounding the resort. The snows came in with a fury in blizzard proportions, and our dorm rooms were so cold. While I was at work during the day, I'd leave my electric hair dryer running to heat my room (not a very smart thing to do; I'm just lucky I didn't burn the place down). Compared to going home, though, not even the cold and the loneliness due to the other kids leaving was so bad. The inevitable day came, however, when the resort was closed for the winter and, regretfully, I knew I had to return home. Mom came after me; and even though she and I had a good time together, it was still a dreadful trip. As the miles quickly shortened between resort and home, I felt doomed. I prayed, "Lord, please give me the strength for what I know is ahead."

Then I was home, and yes, sure enough, dear old Dad thought he'd just take up where he left off. Aside from having to put up with his sick advances all the time, he also started restricting my activities, trying to put curfews on my dating hours, and always acting intolerably jealous of my dates. He made life so miserable. As he had done through the latter years of high school, that winter he even restricted me from going to church choir practice with my mother (something that my mother and I thoroughly enjoyed doing together). We sounded good together and were often asked to sing duets for church; Mom sang a beautiful soprano, and I sang alto. But Dad had other ideas; he wanted me home with him while mother was gone. He'd tell mother I had too many chores, or that he needed help with something and I couldn't go with her. Then, after she had gone, he'd send my brother to his room to do his homework, and he'd make us both an alcoholic drink called a Whiskey Highball (to this day I can't stand the taste or smell of whiskey). He tried to get me drunk so he could do what he wanted without me complaining or refusing. I fought that for a while, but soon I didn't even care. I just tried to get drunk as fast as I could so that I hardly knew what was going on. Hopefully, it would make me numb enough to stand it. It's only by the grace of God that I didn't become an alcoholic, or worse.

It was during these times that I began to have "out of body" experiences. I remember that when he was abusing me, I would all of a sudden float to the ceiling and, looking down, would see it happening to someone else. It was kind of scary at the time, but I guess it was my mental way of handling it and not feeling anything.

But, I also felt a peace, and a curious warmth; I knew that the Lord was watching over me and giving me super strength; because I trusted Him to do just that. It's true, and don't you ever doubt it, when you trust in the Lord, He gives you strength to overcome <u>anything</u>. He'll never let the Devil dish out more than we can take. He watches over us and takes care of our needs and protects us.

As time went on through the winter months, life at home grew more and more intolerable. Dad's improper advances never stopped, he was jealous of my dates and continued to restrict my activities. If that wasn't enough, he and Mom were constantly at each other. Sometimes there were violent fights, and always there was bickering between them. These were all more displays of the complete control he wanted and had over his family. I felt as if I couldn't stand another day there, so I secretly began to make plans to go to California to live with my grandmother (Mom's mother) and look for a job. When I had all the details worked out and my Grandmother was in favor of my living with her, I told my family. Dad objected, of course, and was absolutely furious when Mom bought me a one-way ticket. But, he sent me on my way, saying I could have a few weeks away for a "vacation"; then he'd send me money for me to come home. Little did he realize that I intended to <u>never</u> come back home!

CHAPTER THREE

MARRIAGE, BREAKUPS & MORE SEARCHING

Life in California was such a joy, and I really loved and appreciated getting to know my grandmother, whom I had only been able to visit on vacations as a child about every two years. Fortunately, I was able to find a job right away, too, as a mail clerk in a plant not too far from Grandmother's apartment. It was during that time that I met my first husband (I'll call him Jim) who was seven years older than myself, but who acted much older. He even smoked a pipe and I loved the way he smelled of a really nice pipe tobacco; oddly, it was called "Bourbon Blend". We had spoken at work from the first day; he was the Shipping Clerk and I was the Mail Clerk. Our departments were next door to each other, so we came into contact with each other frequently. Then one day he came into the mail room and, handing me some flowers he had picked on his way to work said, "After work, why don't you show me the way to Grandmother's house, little Red Riding Hood." I was thrilled that this very good-looking "older" man was interested in me, and was impressed with the very romantic way he chose to ask me out. I said YES, of course, and from that day on we were dating and I was feeling on top of the world.

Then, one day my bubble popped again; a letter came from, you guessed it, Dad. He said I'd been in California for six weeks; that was long enough, and now it was time to come home. I wrote back that I was enjoying my stay with Grandma and had a good job with a chance for advancement (I was next in line for keypunch training) and wanted to stay. He wrote back a rather angry letter saying in a very few words to "come home or he'd come after me". Meantime, Jim and I were still dating and, although I didn't love him at the time yet, said, "Yes", when he asked me to marry him. Why? Why not? That way for sure I would never have to go home. At least, if I ever did go home, I'd have a man of my own to protect me. As it turned out, by the time I visited home again, Jim <u>and</u> our new baby son accompanied me.

The first couple of years of married life were pretty good for Jim and I. However, by the time I had suffered an extremely difficult delivery of our first- born son, I wanted nothing to do with the intimacy of marriage. The extremely difficult delivery, coupled with a poor sexual history, resulted in a six-month period of time when I was totally frigid. I admit it, and I know now I should have had some kind of help. However, instead of trying to understand why, possibly getting the counseling we needed and helping his wife through a difficult time, Jim began to come home from his job later and later each night. I felt totally deserted, especially when our son experienced the usual childhood illnesses, and I would be left home with him all evening alone. I'll never forget the night he came home very late and found me asleep in the crib with my son, a tent over us to help him breathe with a vaporizer. He was so frightened from not being able to breathe, that his crying was making him worse; so I crawled in with him.

I finally realized that Jim had a girlfriend (or girlfriends) when I received a hospital bill for his illegitimate child. The bill had been mistakenly sent to our home address rather than to his office as he had instructed. I can't explain how lost and alone I felt at that moment, but in the process, I lost the love and trust that I had grown to feel for him. Somehow, though, we managed to stay together for five more years. I just kept hoping that with the love and understanding of his family he would stop his lying and cheating, but it never happened. During that time we were also blessed with a beautiful daughter, who together with her brother, have been the joys of my life. My children and I have maintained a close relationship over the years for which I am very thankful. I can't imagine what my life would have been like without them. However, Jim's and my marriage was never a close relationship; so, after seven years of marriage, many lies, deceptions, and tears, the union collapsed and we parted and went our separate ways.

You would think after all that I would have learned to be more careful in my choices; but as so many people do, I made the mistake of marrying again, too soon. I know now that it's so important to get counseling and let God heal you of your old wounds before going into another relationship. Countless people (myself included) go from one marriage to another, taking along their old baggage, and never finding out why their relationships aren't successful. Anyway, I made the same mistake, looking for that love and acceptance of a man I could have and hold forever, and who would make everything all right. I didn't take the time to heal first so that I'd have something to offer that man. However, I'm getting ahead of myself.

During Jim's and my separation and divorce, good old Dad showed up again. Here I was, twenty-six years of age, with two lively little children, struggling to make a living on my own, and he showed up to make things more difficult. For the first time in my life I had a really good secretarial job at a local real estate office, was beginning to get some self confidence, and regaining some semblance of self esteem and respect for myself. I even wore my wedding band at work so that the guys in the office would think I was married (that way I figured I could stay clear of any involvements). Believing I was married, the guys at work would sometimes ask as I left for the evening, "What are you fixing your hubby for dinner tonight?" I'd make up something; it was so much simpler that way; no complications, which is what I wanted then.

Then Dad showed up, saying that when the family splits up and goes through hard times they need to seek out other family and stick together. That would have been nice for us; I wanted to believe him. It was easy for me to accept at that time, because I needed to have someone love me and to be there for support. The kids and I were really lonely in that cramped one bedroom apartment. However, I soon learned that it just wasn't going to be that simple. He was the same; he hadn't changed over time as I had hoped he would. One night on a weekend visit to see the kids and I, he made his intentions crystal clear. He was there to "Do me a favor". For the first time in my life I finally voiced my declaration of independence and told him "NO". He tried to argue, but in the end I won and he left me alone. Why hadn't he respected my feelings and stopped long ago? Perhaps now he thought I was old enough that I would press charges for the past. I certainly could have; there are men and women serving years in prison today who have done much less. I don't know; I guess I'll never know. All I do know for sure is that it would have saved a lot of years of heartache if he had stopped years before. I feel that my father's violation and betrayal of my trust in my early years severely affected me, and sent me down a self-destructive path toward years of troubled relationships.

Getting back to my relationship with my second husband, we

married immediately after the divorce with Jim was final. Ted was four and a half years younger than I, and, for the most part, ten times more loving and understanding than Jim. He not only made me feel loved, but he helped me feel like a woman and to think more highly of myself. There would be problems up the road, but I couldn't see anything then but a bright and happy future. He loved the children, and most of the time, when he wasn't drinking, was a good father and guiding influence to them. He didn't drink all the time, but was what I would call a "weekend drinker" or social drinker. He could carry on a job and even take evening classes without letting his drinking interfere. Even when he began to abuse me physically, I was able to overlook it for a long time because I made excuses for him; that it was because of the alcohol. It wasn't until later on when he did it when he was sober that the marriage really suffered. But, during those years, I was very co-dependent, and willing to stand by and take care of my man and actually "fix" him if he wasn't perfect. Anyway, in the meantime, at the kids' request, he adopted them when they were age nine and twelve, just five years after we were married. They had been begging us for sometime to let their new Daddy adopt them. However, even though they were anxious we wanted to be sure that they were old enough to know what it meant, so we made them wait the five years until my son was twelve years old. I'll never forget that day in the judge's chambers. Since my children would have come heir to family money on Jim's side of the family, the judge had to explain to my son (since he was 12) what it would entail. He said, "Son, do you realize that in the future, any money that you would have inherited will not be yours if you let this man adopt you?" My son replied without as much as a pause, "Judge, I think that the love of my new Daddy is worth more than any money I would get." I was so proud of him, these words coming from a 12 year old, and I was happy that he felt that way. We were a very happy family then and believed that we'd always be together.

We began our marriage with honesty, and therefore, I shared my past with my husband. I wanted him to really know me and help me, and I also wanted him to help me with the supervision of our daughter when in the company of my father. The years went by so quickly. The first three years were full of fun, and a mixture of happiness, pain and sorrow, as all marriages are. We experienced so much living and loving during those years.

However, almost immediately, in the first year of our marriage we were faced with standing up to my dad, and "had it out with him". In an earlier conversation that day, Dad had said something that later, as we were driving in the car to meet the folks at a restaurant, had caused my husband and I to get into a very heated argument. We arrived at the restaurant, both biting our tongues and trying to control our anger. It made me more than furious to know that, after all the strife my Dad had caused me in the past, now he had caused this terrible disagreement between us. As we sat at the dining table I was glaring at Dad. He finally noticed and said, "What's wrong?" I said, "You and your big mouth." With that, he flashed me an icy cold glare, his eyes blazing at me, and I knew he was becoming uncontrollably angry himself. One would have to understand the history here to fully appreciate that kind of glare. It was the look that usually struck blind, frozen terror in any of our family that knew him. He held us all in such bondage with his anger and instant temper that always preceded violence. Anyway, I felt an immediate need to beat him to the punch and defend myself, so I broke a glass on the table and started to come at him with it. I know now that I was experiencing what they refer to as "temporary insanity", and I also know that, at that moment, I was capable of killing him. My husband grabbed my hand, preventing me from doing something I'd be sorry for, and told my Dad, "Come on, I want to talk to you outside." Well, of course by this time everyone in the restaurant was aware of a problem, and the waitress called the police. It was quite embarrassing, but we were more concerned with what was going on between the two of them. While my husband and father carried on a very heated conversation in the foyer, shaking their fingers at each other, the police arrived, but didn't interfere at any point. Ted told him he knew what he had done, called him a "baby raper", and told him to never touch his wife or daughter again. We all saw him shaking his finger at my Dad to enforce what he was telling him. They returned to the dining room and nothing else was said. However, as a result of that confrontation, my father referred to me as a "traitor" with "traitorous tendencies" and alienated us for the next five years, never letting my mother even mention my name. He'd say, "Sandy? Who's that?" The only advantage during those years was the fact that we were living clear across the country in the Southwest and didn't have to be in contact with him if we didn't want to. Mom would call us when she could when he wasn't around, and even visited us a few times, but we didn't go to their home or see him for five years.

After a few years we decided to move back to my home state and put down some roots. Ted had secured a wonderful job just 50 miles from my parent's home. When we got settled, I started taking the kids to church, although I had not attended for years and had really been away from the Lord and backslidden a lot. My husband wouldn't attend with us at first; he never thought he needed church. I think the only reason he believed in the Lord was because he was afraid not to (afraid that he wouldn't go to heaven).

One day after we had gone to church and he was alone, Ted must have felt the prompting of the Lord while he was lying on the couch in the living room. He turned the TV on, and while watching a Christian broadcast, he heard the salvation message in a way he had never heard it before. He decided then and there to give his heart to the Lord, and was instantly filled with the Holy Spirit and was speaking in tongues. From that time on he was a changed person. Determined to live his life for Christ, he gave up drinking altogether, and decided he wanted to do something constructive for the Lord.

Then something "constructive" came up. The Pastor of our small church needed a couple to serve as youth ministers, and although we had never done anything like that, we agreed. It was a very small church, and no one else wanted to do it, so, since we were willing, we were IT (no training or experience, just a willingness and excitement at the thought of helping the kids). It was a wonderful way to be with our own kids and participate with them in their activities. The next four and a half years were filled with lots of fun, adventure and many side trips. It was rewarding beyond belief. We started a puppet ministry with the kids, took all kinds of trips to Christian concerts, tried to help the kids with their problems, and all the while struggling against Satan and his constant bombardments of spiritual warfare. There was always an extra kid or two at our table in those days, and in later years I missed that for a long time. All during those years, no matter how the enemy came against us, "United we stood". It was only when the enemy was able to separate us as a family (divide and conquer) that he nearly destroyed us all. That is why to this day I do not believe in families being separated, for jobs or for any other reason. There are just too many temptations out there, and when you are lonely, you are vulnerable and the enemy (Satan) can come against you. Unhappily, we were not able to keep our family together, as during the separation, we both were tempted by the Devil and fell into sin. Too much happened and we were never able to salvage what we once had. But, that's another story and will probably be in my next book.

I just want you to be able to see through these examples of failed marriages, just how much I was affected later on by the abuses throughout my childhood. It seems in all my relationships of the past I was always trying to "fix" people. I was very co-dependent and ended up "fixing" and putting three husbands through school! Did I say three? Yes, I did, read on.

That last family separation and break up I told you about was in 1983. My children had just left the nest, my son just three years before to the U.S. Coast Guard; my daughter the year of our breakup (to be married and have my first grandchild). Except for the bonus of my grandson, it was a pretty devastating time. All in a little over a year I lost my home, my husband, and my children. At least it feels as if you've lost them when they first leave the nest! However, I am very fortunate, because I have a wonderful relationship with my children, and over the years they have given me seven beautiful grandchildren. In the meantime, "Grandma" had to start life over (at 42 years of age), and what a time of rebirth! My daughter and I had moved to Alaska to be closer to my son stationed there with the Coast Guard. Both my kids met their spouses soon after, and Mom was alone again.

When I visited my son's Assembly of God Church, I met Mark, a very nice, gentle, Alaskan man, who liked me as much as I liked him. But, again, he was a needy man that I could "fix". He was 12 years younger than I, and had not yet established a career (little did I know what was ahead, and that I would put this one through years of schooling, too). Even though there was a significant age difference, and he was actually a friend of my son's, we were always being thrown together by circumstances. Even at 27, Mark was the oldest member of the youth group, and I, being an "old" youth pastor, always felt more comfortable being part of and helping in the youth group. We became friends, attending church together, going hunting, boating, hiking and fishing. The age difference didn't even seem to matter, and it was evident from the start that we both loved the great outdoors. After knowing each other for two years, we realized one day that we didn't want to live the rest of our lives alone or without each other, so he asked me to marry him. We had a small quiet wedding in the church where we had met, with just his family and our closest friends in attendance (my children had already moved away from the area, and my parents were too far away to come; besides, they had already attended two of my weddings). Over the next decade we had a very full life together, all of its ups and downs, joys and sorrows, and constant changes. He was never able to hold a job for very long, and wanted so desperately to be in law enforcement. He worked at the local pulp mill until it closed. I ended up working while he went through years of classes (some out of town and, in one case, off the island) and police academies. He tried so hard, but was never able to reach his goals. I ended up working a full time job, running a bed and breakfast out of our home, and selling cosmetics and giving skin care classes in the evenings when I wasn't doing anything else . . .Ha! I didn't feel that he helped me enough with everything I was trying to do to maintain this "survival" mode. For a long time he refused to help in the upkeep of the home and bed and breakfast that was "our" responsibility, and I began to have deep resentments and went into a depression that led to anxiety. We went through some counseling together, but I had lost respect for him through it all and couldn't bear to stay in the marriage. I really felt that physically and mentally the marriage was killing me, and I had so many anxiety attacks that I never knew when one would hit me. I just knew I had to get out. But we tried a temporary two months separation and went through counseling anyway. When we got back together for a few months, he slipped right back into the old pattern, and we never could really get it back together. I closed the bed and breakfast and moved downstairs into the guest room.

In the past I had never given myself time in between relationships to get that total healing that only God can give. So this time, I determined to do just that. I admit, although I don't like to think about this part, but I actually had to "harden" my heart (just temporarily) in order to do what I knew I had to do. After all, Mark was basically a sweet guy, or I never would have fallen in love with him in the first place. But, he refused to really grow up and know what was important, and too much had happened. Again, I had lost all respect and love for the man I had married. To accomplish my goal, first of all I needed to distance myself from all the hurts I had experienced. Deciding to take advantage of an early retirement incentive plan, I went through a third divorce that was final (on my birthday) just two weeks before my retirement, and headed out five days later on the first ferry for the mainland. There I would be closer to family and be able to go to church and heal. The trip "home" was delightfully refreshing.

I didn't see much of my folks during that time. I think Mom was always dreading a confrontation between Dad and myself, so she'd just rather not get together. We didn't know then, but Dad was in the early to mid stages of dementia, and over the next couple of years would go down hill fast. There was no sense in raking up the past and talking with him then, as he had really closed the door on any kind of reconciliation years before when I was living in Alaska. During the time that I was in Alaska and married to Mark, there *was* a time of confrontation. I had attempted to make him own up to his responsibility for the abuse, ask my forgiveness, and make his amends with God. In the following chapter I will share with you how that all unfolded and how we handled it and, ultimately, lived with the results.

CHAPTER FOUR

THE CONFRONTATION

This is how it all came about: the second opportunity to make him own up to his abuse; and I'm very glad I had that opportunity, because then I knew that he had every chance at that moment to ask my forgiveness, and get right with the Lord. This is how it happened.

Mark and I had been talking to the folks on the phone, and I had asked them if Mom could go to Hawaii with all of us gals in the family. Mom had always wanted to go there, since way before their 25th wedding anniversary, and Dad had always found other things to do and other places to go. But when I asked, he said, "Your mother and I usually do things like that together, and I resent the fact that you asked her." I told him it was because he didn't want to go and she still very much did. Well, we got into an argument and it brought out all the resentment in me for the way he had cheated our family out of so much over the years. I told him that he was selfish as usual and that he owed me an apology and needed to ask my forgiveness for what he had done. He told me he didn't know what I was talking about. So I asked him, "Do you deny that you sexually abused me as a child, and molested me all throughout my childhood?" Guess I didn't feel like "mincing words" and got right to the point. He was very angry and, lashing out, hung up on me. Well, I was immediately afraid that he would do something to hurt my mother, and I was tempted to call the police there and send them over to protect her. But thankfully, the Lord spoke to my heart and told me to call our best friends and ask them to pray with us. We got them on the phone and began to pray, the four of us, that the Lord would protect her and work this thing out. We had no more than hung up from that phone call and the phone rang. It was my Dad. He said, "Your mother tells me I owe you an apology." I said, "Yes, it has been a long time coming." I thought that he was finally going to say he was sorry, but instead he said something that will stick in my mind for all eternity. He said, "Well, dear, let me tell you this much, I'm sorry for anything that you *think* I did." It blew me away! In other words, he was not remorseful at all, and certainly didn't need or want my forgiveness. He did say one thing more, though, that gave me hope and another window of opportunity. He said, "Why don't you write me a letter and explain everything." I told him I would, and I have included it as part of this story, as a letter of sorts to all abusers, so they may know that they have a responsibility to ask forgiveness: from the victim and especially from God.

MY LETTER TO DAD (written on October 22, 1990)

"Dearest Dad,

I praise God for you and Mom, and for what our Lord is doing in all our lives! Yesterday was hard for all of us, and today wasn't much better, but we all took a big step to bringing our family closer than maybe we've ever been before. It is a turning point for us, and a new beginning. You asked me to write you a long letter, and, with God's help, I will try to write this letter as the Spirit leads me. I have prayed about this, and pray you will accept it in the love it is offered.

As you know, there are many things one can't say in a brief phone call, but there are things that need to be said to bring you to total repentance and deliverance. In any healing process, the truth stirs us up, bringing out many emotions. I ask that you just read it in a place alone, with an open mind and heart. I promise to speak in truth from my heart, with the sole purpose of bringing you to remembrance of the things I have asked the Lord to forgive you for.

I don't know whether or not you have ever thought about this, but our family has been what is called a *dysfunctional* family. What made us dysfunctional was the state of "denial" we were always in. We denied, or kept silent, about our abuse because of the fear bondage we were held under. I know you loved us Dad, but maybe something in your own childhood or past filled you with such a rage that you had to vent it someway. It came out in the form of abuse, and you were

31

abusive to all of us: Mom and my little brother were abused verbally and emotionally, and you abused me sexually ever since I was three years old. Your anger and temper held us all in a paralyzed state and kept us from sharing our inner most thoughts and needs with you. The Word of God says, that to overcome this a transformation is needed, brought about by a renewing of the mind. The place to start is with repentance and faith in Christ to remove and overcome the rage experience. I wish you could seek out a spirit-filled fellowship or pastor to help you pray this through; but I will be praying for you. The fruits of your deliverance will be evidenced by your total lack of anger, and you will be free from it; you will **want** to ask our forgiveness.

These are some good scriptures to show why repentance is so important:

Exodus 20:5: For I the Lord thy God am a jealous God, visiting the iniquity of the fathers upon the children unto the **third and fourth generation** of them that hate me; and showing mercy unto thousands of them that love me and keep my commandments." *Hate* here means those who do not follow his commandments.

Also please read these scriptures:

Romans 13:1-3; I Peter 2:13-14; Luke 17:2; and best yet: Romans 12:2. Dad, please do read these and it will help you understand more fully why we all need sincere repentance. I have dropped to my knees at the feet of Jesus many times, and He is always faithful to forgive and to renew us with a right spirit.

You may break God's laws, but disobedience will result in the wreckage of your life and of those you improperly involve. It is impossible to involve yourself sexually without involving the spiritual nature of your partner and yourself. One may try to turn off this spiritual involvement, but they succeed only in hardening and callusing the spirit, which is the worst effect of all. You then become guilty of tampering with the spiritual core of a person. The scars from this kind of involvement are ugly, deep, and long lasting. God cares too much about all of His children to leave such tampering and spiritual abuse unpunished. This is why you need to ask God for forgiveness. Ephesians 6: "And, ye fathers, provoke not your children to wrath; but bring them up in the nurture and admonition of the Lord."

Dad, I used to have a terrible temper when I was raising the kids, and would throw things out of anger. It was the way I vented pent-up feelings I held inside. However, I was delivered from it and now am spirit controlled, free from rage. It's okay to feel a "righteous anger" and to use it as Jesus did to accomplish good, but that's what I meant when I said, "You can tell by the **fruits** your deliverance displays. You can see and feel the difference in a totally free, repentant person; their whole countenance is new. Dad, that is the repentant peace I pray for you."

Love, Your Daughter Sandy

I never received an answer to that letter, and no signs of any kind that he had read it. He told me a few years later when the subject came up again, that he had asked the Lord to forgive him, and that was all he felt was necessary. Sadly, he went to his grave never having said he was sorry or asking any of us for forgiveness.

I realize now that the title of my book is a little misleading, as if I could intercede for my father and ask God to forgive him. That was a child's concept and born out of youthful wishing. It says in God's word that he gives each person "a measure of faith" on which to act, and that it is "up to us to work out our own salvation". Therefore, I know now that I could not be responsible for "saving" my Dad, only God can do that. Dad would have only had to ask. Jesus said that, "No one goes to the Father except through me." I hope and I pray that he did.

However, over the next few years, through God's help, much prayer, going through the steps of forgiveness, and learning to have "tough love" with myself, I've come to feel a real peace. The key to total healing is forgiveness. Later on in Appendix C of this book I will give you the steps to overcome your hurts and disappointments of the past and truly forgive. I also had to come to the place where I asked myself, "Just how long are you going to let this thing keep you down; keep you from living a life of love and trust?" That is "tough love" with yourself. You make up your mind, that with God's help, you are going to overcome and be victorious. I'm so thankful I have you in my life, Lord.

Furthermore, in my sunset years, God has blessed me with a fourth and final husband, who is a Christian and loves the Lord and me, and doesn't have to be put through school! He is retired after having been a junior high school teacher for thirty-one years. He has promised me that the only school he will ever be interested in is one to help him restore old boats and cars in our retirement. I was so impressed when his two granddaughters "found me" for him (they went looking for a short lady for their short grandpa on the Internet, and found me). Yes, I admit that I got a little fearful that I was going to be by myself for the rest of my life, so I put an ad on the Yahoo Personals. The girls answered it, telling him at the same time what they were doing. They were visiting him, and one day while he was busy with a project, they got busy on the computer. They interrupted him to tell him they wanted to find a lady friend for him on Yahoo, and would it be ok. In his busyness, he just answered quickly, "Oh, I guess so." Then they asked him, "Grandpa, what are you looking for in a lady?" And he answered them, "Well, not someone too young (we had both been that route), and someone not too tall (he is 5'4", and I am 5'2" tall). So they went to work writing an ad for him. I got home from work that night and, checking my email messages, found the sweetest letter from two young girls (I found out later that they were 16 and 19 years old). I thought to myself, this must be one special man to have his granddaughters think so highly of him and want to do this for him. They said in their letter that "We want you to meet our Grandpa. He's a really cool guy who likes to travel EVERYWHERE." Well, this appealed to me, so I answered their letter because I felt that he must be as "cool" as they said he was if they would do that for their grandpa. I told them, "Don't find your Grandpa anymore dates until I have a chance to check him out." I'm very fortunate that he is an extremely family oriented man with a wonderful family who has shown me both love and acceptance. Both of us had come out of unhappy marriages, had a time of healing, and wanted more out of life. This time, though, we gave it two years, a lot of good talks, prayer and counseling, and really getting to know each other. We have a lot in common and are enjoying our families and friends, our projects (he has one after another), traveling together, and life in general.

"My Story" would not be complete, however, if I didn't share with you the happiness my mother has also found. During our courtship, we had the opportunity to introduce my mother to a gentleman we had met while eating at a local diner. We had talked with him a few times, and one time when the diner was full, he invited us to sit with him at his table. The more we talked with this gentleman, the more we thought what a good influence he would be on my Mom. Although he was older (92 at the time) he was a go-getter who had his own cell phone, computer and a pickup truck. Then one day we invited them both over for dinner (on his birthday) so they could meet. To make a long story short, they dated for a few months, and then on my mother's 83rd birthday, he proposed to her. They announced it at a family gathering on our deck to celebrate her birthday. I'll never forget the shy way she told us that he had asked her to be his wife; then paused while we all sucked in our breath in anticipation. When my niece asked, "Well, Grandma, what did you say?" she replied happily, "Well, I said Yes, of course." Then **they** beat **us** to the alter by one month!! I guess at their ages they thought they didn't want to waste any time. They were the oldest couple their pastor had ever married. My brother and I, along with our spouses, and my two new brothers and three new sisters (my new Dad's children) and their spouses enjoyed sharing their simple ceremony in the living room of their lovely home. Mom & Dad looked so happy, and we were happy for them.

As an added bonus, we finally got Mom to Hawaii recently, to fulfill her lifelong dream of over 70 years. Mom is now 87 and Dad celebrated his 96th birthday on Easter while we were in Hawaii. We have all been married for over three years now; our lives together are wonderfully full, and I want to thank the Lord for our healing and happiness. He has walked with me all these years, and sometimes he has carried me (as in Footprints). I will praise Him forever, and be eternally grateful for his love and protection all the way. I love you so much, Lord, for who you are and all that you have done in our lives.

CHAPTER FIVE

FEELINGS OF GUILT, SHAME & SECRECY

The worst part of being an incest victim for many people is the damage done to their self-esteem; negative feelings about themselves which linger long after the actual incest is over. In some cases, such as my own, these are feelings that one never gets a break from for many years. If it goes on throughout an individual's entire childhood, rather than a single isolated event, the traumatic affect of these feelings of low self esteem are compounded and even more severe, and seemingly unending and unendurable. Without intervention, sexual abuse can lead to sexual problems in adulthood. Studies are finding that many child molesters, violent criminals and prostitutes were victims of sexual abuse as children.

Because incest victims rarely talk about their abuse with others who have had similar experiences, they often feel isolated and ashamed. For this reason, among other reasons, group therapy sessions with other victims has been found to be most beneficial, not to mention soothing, to those who have been abused. This will be discussed in greater detail in my next chapter on Group Therapy.

Guilt

Looking back over the years I can see now how much guilt I really did suffer. I'm just so thankful that I did have my Lord to tell these things, too, because He was the <u>only</u> one I *thought* I could share this guilt with for well over fifteen years! I shared everything with Him in a diary as a child. Years later I found the poem "Father, Forgive My Father" tucked in the pages of that diary, and it reminded me of the promise I made to Him to share my experiences with others in a book when I was grown up.

I believe my greatest guilt feelings stemmed from the way I felt I was betraying my mother. Even though my father had threatened me with death, or the death of my family, I still blamed myself to a certain extent for permitting it to go on. I have to admit, if I'm to be completely honest, that some of my guilt, probably a great deal, resulted from the hate I felt for both my father and my mother. Don't misunderstand, I always loved them because they were my parents, and you're supposed to love and obey your parents. But, at the same time, I hated my father for what he was doing to me, and I hated my mother because I always had in the back of my mind that she <u>must</u> know what was happening, and if she did, she was allowing it to continue. She was allowing him to hurt me. During therapy sessions they told me that in the process of recovery, I must confront her and make her own up to her responsibility.

I did that, and it was very hard. One day when we were talking about the past, I shared with Mom how I felt, and that I had been going for therapy and what they had said. Mom was very uncomfortable, and said, "Well, I never knew anything was wrong until that camping trip." That kind of threw me, because during my childhood we had gone on many camping trips. So I said to her, "Which one was that?" Then she described to me the trip we had taken to the west coast, tenting in various campgrounds. I pinpointed it to the time period just before I entered junior high school (I would have been 13 years old that summer). She described to me what had happened that night. As I said, we were "tenting", so at each campground, we would set up the tent, and Dad would arrange the sleeping bags across the back section of the tent. He always placed Mom on the outside, him next, mine was after that, and my brother's was on the other outside wall of the tent. Well, Mom had awakened in the night to find Dad messing around with me, and angrily asked him, "What do you think you're doing?" Dad just pretended that he was doing something in his sleep, and so everyone went back to sleep after that, except me. I lay awake for hours after wondering what would happen next. When I remembered back to that event, and realized how long ago it had been, I was enraged. In other words, she had let me endure this torment of abuse for the rest of my junior high school AND high school years! Six long, long, years! There had even been times when she went on trips with her girl friends and left me home alone with Dad and my brother. They kidded me for a long time about how I cooked "cinders" of bacon for them (I wasn't very adapt at cooking at that age). I didn't mind cooking or cleaning for them, but those were pretty terrible times, when the nights were so unending. I hated to see her go on those trips, but I was also glad in a way that she could get out from under his cranky ways for awhile, reasoning that she needed to get away for a break. I think now that those thoughts were evidence of how co-dependent I had already become. Wanting to "fix" things and "take care" of people despite my own feelings. Anyway, when I shared with Mom how resentful I was of those times and her not sticking up for me, she said, "Well, honey, you know that I was afraid of him, too." That is how he held us all in bondage, with earth shaking, paralyzing fear.

There were times, many times, when I felt my only ally was God. I can't even remember how I handled everything up until the summer before my 8th grade year when I really met Christ in a real way and was *born again*. It must have been through the fervent prayers of my maternal grandmother, as she told me years later that she had always prayed for my protection and my salvation. I can tell you this: If you have a God fearing, praying Grandmother,

Satan might just as well give up, because you're going to be alright, and you will be set aside for His kingdom. I'm hoping that if my grandchildren ever read this, they will remember that this Grandma is praying for them wherever they are.

Getting back to the summer before 8th grade. It was at that time I fully accepted Christ into my life and was able to give the problem to Him. I remember the occasion vividly, as if it were yesterday, perhaps because it was like the first ray of hope in my young life. The youth of our church had traveled to a summer church camp in the Cascades of Washington State. It was beautiful there in the woods, peaceful and refreshing; especially to me at that time. After all, it was a retreat of sorts, a place to escape my father's constant harassment. One night, after we had been there a few days, I had a most meaningful, memorable and absolutely beautiful experience during campfire vespers. As the firelight illuminated each young face around the campfire, each child shared how he or she felt about their life and their relationship with the Lord. Up until this time I had always attended Sunday school and church, but had never met the Lord face to face. But that night, I remember the awe and love of the Lord. It was like He had his all-protecting hand on my life, and I finally gave my life to Him. I felt warm all over, and there was a glow coming down from the sky that wasn't from the campfire. There was a feeling of love in my heart for other people that I had never felt. It's hard to explain, but I was truly born again, and I knew it! That meant a tremendous burden was almost instantly lifted from me. I finally had someone to tell all my problems to, a comforter in time of trouble, a friend when I needed (which was all the time), and someone who I felt sure, would get me through these terrible trying times. I know without a doubt that I am sane and a whole person today because of the Lord's loving guidance and protection; free from harsh repercussions such as prostitution, drugs, and self destructive tendencies, etc. that others have suffered. If it hadn't been for the Lord, my own personal savior (and yours if you will let Him be) this author would not be here today, giving you these words. He took me out of my lonely suffering and bondage and gave me a promise of better days ahead. I think the words of the song following say it all: "Thru it all I've learned to trust in Jesus, thru it all I've learned to trust in God. I've learned to depend upon His word. You're never alone when you trust in Him; God will never fail you or forsake you."

However, on the other hand, if a young person doesn't have a firm faith in the Lord, or some professional person trained to listen, which enables her to talk it over with someone and unload the terrible burden of guilt she feels, it leads to an even greater feeling of low self esteem----SHAME!

Shame

Webster's Dictionary defines shame very well, and I will reiterate in an attempt to depict exactly how it feels: "A painful emotion caused by consciousness of guilt, shortcoming, or impropriety; dishonor, disgrace; something that brings strong regret or reproach." That's it in a nutshell: all the terrible, repressing, degrading feelings of SHAME. If you have never had these kinds of feelings, it is probably hard to imagine how shame can make you shrink from society. A good example of such a situation was a victim who had been sexually abused as a youngster and later reported, "I always skipped classes that required close contact or focused attention on me. I was good in any subject that didn't require me to perform. I skipped English on the days we were to give a speech or read aloud. I couldn't stand up in front of a class; I was afraid they would see something or, if I opened my mouth, everything about my father would come pouring out. I never asked any questions for the same reason, and for fear of sounding stupid." These feelings also depict the lack of self-confidence and of low self esteem that most victims usually experience. Unfortunately, most suffer these feelings throughout their entire lifetime.

I can remember feeling such shame so intensely at school that it made me terribly inhibited; not only among my friends, but also with teachers. It was so bad one day that it made me forget an entire poem that I had committed to memory. I knew that poem backwards and forwards and had recited it in front of my family and in front of the mirror like they tell you to do. However, when I stood up in front of the class to recite, all the feelings of guilt, shame and downright inadequacy surfaced, and all I could do was stare blankly as my face I am sure turned a brilliant crimson. That teacher had me stay after school that day, and I remember vividly his question, "Are you afraid of me? Is that why you couldn't recite today?" He paused for a moment; then continued, "You sit here in my class all day, just sitting there. You never contribute or raise your hand to give an answer! Sometimes I wonder what goes on in your head, girl." My feelings today are that he didn't wonder quite enough. To have asked such questions, he must have had some inkling or suspicion of my feelings, and he should have taken it a step further.

Listen, people, this is <u>very</u> important. If teachers and people in general were a little more perceptive at times, they could be a lot more help to their students. Teachers and all who read this, please refer to this book's Appendix A: "The Signs That Spell Abuse", where I delve deeper into how to recognize the sexually abused child and what signs to look for. It could save the life of one of your students. As it was in my case, it wouldn't have taken much more urging or prodding at that particular time for me to have blurted out the whole sad story. Perhaps then I could have received some real counseling and inevitably been helped at an earlier age. But then I had it imbedded in my brain by my father that you didn't confide such things to anyone, <u>not anyone</u>, because serious consequences would result. He said you couldn't trust anyone with family information, and that it would just mean that our family would be split apart and they would take him away. Then he threatened that eventually he would fool the psychiatrists and would get out and come back and shoot the whole bunch of us. So, I resorted to keeping it quiet to protect my family, and buried myself in SECRECY.

Secrecy

Except for God, my friend and confidant, no one knew of my predicament for well over fifteen years. That is a long time to keep a secret! If only someone had told me (or I had asked) there never was a need for complete secrecy. But I felt for my own safety and that of my family's there was. I know now that there are trained professional people in our society who are equipped to help us, and more than happy to help us. (See Appendix B: "List of Agencies To Contact For Help" in the back of this book). If only I'd confided in my pastor. At that time when there were so few institutions available for help, he would have been my best source for guidance. I was just too afraid to tell *anyone,* for fear my father would destroy our

47

family before the authorities could take the necessary precautions to protect us. Just the thought and threat of family separation has been known to keep many victims silent; this very fact is a tool that many perpetrators use to keep their secret. As I stated before, even if they did take him away to give him help, I believed what he told me (because kids do tend to believe what their folks tell them) that he would come back and kill the whole bunch of us.

I didn't feel I could even confide in my two best girl friends, whom I had known since our first year of junior high school, because I didn't want them to know my shame and how "dirty" I was. As one other victim reported: "Gym class was always a great source of anxiety for me. I wouldn't undress in front of the others; I was afraid they would see something if they saw my body. To me, it seemed my body was always dirty and ugly and a source of shame. I felt fat, even though I was skinny; I thought I looked different, even though I didn't." I know just what she meant, because I felt the same way! It is for this very reason that so many of our young girls are anorexic or have other eating disorders. And, it is one way they can control some area of their life.

Gym class was the time of day I dreaded most. I was known as "The Princess" or "The Troublemaker", and my gym teacher did not hesitate to refer to me as such in front of the class. Here again, teachers, stop, look and listen to your students. Watch for these very evident signs! I didn't want to dress down or shower in the usual gang shower, but always requested the private stall showers for the girls who were having their periods. The teacher would make a big deal of it and say, "Does the Princess want her privacy **again**?" You would have thought that might have tipped her off, but it didn't. That's what I mean by teachers needing to be more perceptive when they see or hear something like this. So gym class was a real nightmare. But, I just kept silent, and continued to pal around with the same friends, feeling like I was not as good as or as "clean" as the rest of our bunch. I felt older and used beyond my young years.

The closest I ever came to telling anyone about what was happening in my life was during the time I was going steady with David, the boy I dated for two years during high school. The fact that I enjoyed a steady relationship with a boy during that period of my life is further evidence of God's love and guidance. Most girls in similar situations would either shy away from boys altogether, or go completely in the other direction, becoming "wild" and leading very promiscuous lifestyles. David was, for the most part, usually pretty understanding about most things, and a few times I was very tempted to unload the burden on him. For one thing: it wasn't fair!! I knew at a young age that I didn't want to lead a promiscuous life, and also knew I wanted to save physical love for marriage. But, we were young and in love, and many times almost gave in to the desires we felt for each other. At those times I was particularly vulnerable to feelings of being cheated, and the old Devil would get a temporary grip on me and say, "What are you saving it for? You know what you have to go home to. Why should you cheat yourself and your boyfriend by holding back honest feelings, when you have to go home to such abuse?" That is where I believe God really helped me. Because I had put my faith and trust in Him, I believe he showed me how to deal with my feelings, and through prayer I was able to conquer the Devil's temptations and suggestions, unburdening all this guilt, shame and secrecy on an ever loving, forgiving and consoling source, our God!

CHAPTER SIX

INCEST, THE GREAT TABOO

Incest, a major form of child sexual abuse, has been called the "last taboo" (I call it the Great Taboo), but its taboo status hasn't kept it from happening. For too long, people have feared the word. Victims have suffered quietly, surrounded by the darkness of guilt, shame and secrecy. Now, as a result of strengthened child abuse laws, new state statutes, and persistent public education efforts, reported cases of incest and childhood sexual abuse are on the rise. Incidents are surfacing, people's stories are being told, and help is being given.

According to the ABC television news program, "Children At Risk" which aired April 26th, 2005, there is a plan underway to overhaul child abuse laws in general. They also referred to sexual child abuse as the "national epidemic" we know it is. According to this broadcast, the City of Pittsburgh, PA has stepped out and become a model for the rest of the country. We can only hope that other US cities will follow in their footsteps.

Also, many new laws to support victims were designed and supported in the state of California. One of the most important was to eliminate the statute of limitations for criminal prosecution in cases of incest and child sexual abuse. Claire Reeves, through MASA (Mothers Against Sexual Abuse), worked tirelessly to allow redress for victims in the courts in California. Reeves also worked closely with Attorney General Dan Lungren to pass legislation for a 900 telephone number that would identify registered sex offenders in the state of California. Alert registries are noted at the end of Chapter 8.

The FBI and other sources I have researched estimate that one in every three females and one in every five males will be sexually assaulted before they graduate from high school. One of the worst kinds of crimes is sexual child abuse or incest within what should be a comforting, trusting family circle. How would you feel if you were a child, and someone you trusted came into your life and stole your self confidence and self esteem, ruined your trust in others, and crushed you repeatedly until you were bruised and paralyzed with fear? If it was a thief in the night and he broke into our home and stole precious possessions, we wouldn't hesitate to report it. And then to make matters worse what if the abuser was someone in your family, like your own father or a brother or even your uncle or grandfather? I know so many young women who are suffering today because their brother, grandfather or father crossed that line. Some of them are in prison today, but many others are not paying for the pain they inflicted.

Incest is bondage, its closely guarded secret holding its victims more tightly than any other; in chains from which they cannot easily escape. There seems to be no escape from the guilt, shame, secrecy, confusion and fear that envelope them, creating a dark dungeon. As one person testified: "I was a prisoner for years later; long after the years of physical abuse ended." I know how she felt, because I always felt like I was sinking into a miry bog; that no one could pull me out. It seemed like an unending, miserable existence. But, then one day I felt *rescued,* that someone did care and would pull me out. As a child we always went to church; I had been through Sunday school and had a basic knowledge and belief in God. But, I found a new strength and comfort in my relationship with the Lord at the church camp evening campfire vesper service the summer before eighth grade. I was led in the sinner's prayer, and turned my life over to Him that night. That was the real turning point; I felt rescued, and I thank God for reaching down and saving me.

What IS Incest?

What exactly IS incest? Many people have it confused with sexual child abuse in general and lump the two together. To put it bluntly, incest is sexual intercourse between two people who are related. The word "incest" includes many sexual acts such as inappropriate touching, molestation, sexual exhibitionism, oral or anal sex, masturbation in front of a child, photographing nude children, and child prostitution, since these too, leave deep, long lasting emotional scars. Let me make this clear: I'm not referring to normal physical affection between parents and kids when I speak of sexual abuse. Some of the *all-essential* ingredients in a loving family are good-natured fooling around such as plenty of hugs, kisses, and hand-holding. Children and parents would miss out on a whole lot without such healthy affection; a warm sense of security that God wants for our families. Incest is something totally different!

Perpetrators, or abusers, don't stick out in a crowd. On the contrary, friends, families and coworkers usually see most abusers as quite "normal". Sadly, we live in a time and society in which some individuals consider it is their right to force themselves on unsuspecting children, especially in their families. Because of the child's trusting relationship with them, abuse by stepparents, aunts, uncles, older siblings, or close family friends also falls into this category. Child sexual abuse is a crime! It occurs when someone uses a child or young person for his or her own sexual gratification. When the abuse takes place in the family, it is called "incest".

Sexual abuse happens in families of every social, economic and ethnic background; *not* just among the poor and unreligious. Many molesters appear to be upstanding members of their community and church (my father, for instance, was a Sunday school teacher, deacon, and an elder of our church, and a professional person who was well thought of in his field). Sadly, most cases go unreported, so the full extent of this problem (epidemic) remains hidden.

One out of every ten homes is not a home, but the cell of an incest victim. As was stated earlier in "My Story", a child waits in terror night after night, hoping against experience that her father will not come to her room that night; that her young body and her trust will not be violated again. Such statements have become almost commonplace in recent media campaigns. Shocking us out of the longstanding misconception that a powerful taboo renders incestuous sexual abuse so improbable that it can be safely dismissed, such statements have served a vital purpose. At the same time, statements made in these media campaigns, as well as in popular magazines, newspapers, and the many pamphlets now on display in medical and public health settings, are giving rise to a new set of myths.

Even the most careful studies of incest families have usually relied on a very small number of cases, since, as stated before, only about 50% of actual cases of incest are reported. Further, most of these studies have focused only on victims discovered in certain settings (children's hospitals, shelters for battered children, or police files, for example), cases which may be wholly unrepresentative of incest families in the society at large. Typical, too, are accounts of the "incest scenario" based solely upon victim self-reports, a datum precariously dependent upon the victim's memory, candor, and childhood grasp of the situation. After reading one or a few such reports, journalists have written many newspaper and magazine articles elevating these often misleading portrayals to the status of universals. Sexual abuse pamphlets prepared by national health agencies are frequently based on evidence nearly as limited. However, we now know that the following statistics (recorded in 1999 & 2000) represent at least minimal numbers.

According to published statistics by the National Crime Victimization Survey (1999 & 2000) of the known sexual abuse, 75% or more is committed by the children's own parents. Victims are usually girls ranging in age between 8 and 12, with 30% under the age of seven. However, girls are not alone in being victimized, and there are many boys who are abused as well. As I stated before, one girl out of three and one boy out of five will be sexually assaulted by the age of 18. The average period of abuse is seven years (mine, unfortunately lasted 15 years). It is a well-known fact that those years result in horrendous after affects. Our prisons today are full of victims. Recent studies show that way over 50% of prison inmates interviewed had been molested as children.

Who Are These Abusers?

A really startling published fact is that "90% of the victims of child sexual abuse know their abusers—they are the fathers, mothers, siblings, close relatives, friends, or other caretakers of children. They are rarely the monsters we imagine lurking in the corners of our playgrounds and parks." Copyright Stop It Now! (2003). Reprinted with permission from Stop It Now!. www.stopitnow.org.

They are people the victim trusts, and at least 50% or more of sexual abuse occurs within the family. Some characteristics of an abuser might be one who:

- Was raised with low nurture in the home
- Has low self-esteem
- Was sexually abused when younger
- Was not loved as a child
- Has emotional upheaval (death in the family, loss of job, etc.)
- Has unresolved anger toward a controlling person or situation

The abuser is usually the person who spends most of the time with the child. The abuser does not hate the child, but, on the contrary, usually loves the child very much. They tend to abuse the child to destroy that part of themselves that they hate, or they abuse to control some part of their life.

Studies way back in the 1970s and 1980s stated that there were probably more than 10,000,000 Americans who had been involved in incest. Recent studies prove that the actual number is much higher, and they are from every geographical area, from every cultural, racial, religious, and educational background. They also come from every profession imaginable, such as lawyers, policemen, doctors, secretaries, artists, and merchants. They are married and they are four times or more divorced. They are heterosexual, bisexual, and homosexual. They are leading otherwise productive lives, and some have been convicted of murder. Some are emotionally stable and others have multiple personalities. In other words, these people only have one thing in common: INCEST. Unfortunately, with these people, incest is their way of life; they are totally consumed with the activities of their lifestyle. Incest involves and touches at least a third of the American population, and is not, as many believed in the past, confined to isolated and perverted events that happen in some dark alley. According to studies just thirty years ago, problems of sexual abuse of children was of unknown national dimensions, but it was suspected even then that the numbers of incidence of abuse were <u>many times larger</u> than reported. It is certain now that everything we've read in the past about the battered child epidemic in general has been extremely underestimated, and a large portion of the problem is incest. In other words, the occurrence of incest is of epidemic proportion, and so much more prevalent than most people ever realized or cared to admit. We know now that previous estimates that it was just that "one-in-a-million" child affected by incest, were sorely miscalculated; recent studies prove that thought to be only wishful thinking.

As Claire R. Reeves stated in her book "Childhood-It Should Not Hurt", "Since 1993, I have been telling colleagues and friends that the movement to make pedophilia an alternate lifestyle is upon us. They have uniformly reacted with vehement denial and outrage, assuring me that good folks would never let this happen. Well, good folks, you had better become pro-activists and advocates for child victims of sexual abuse, because it is already happening." Copyright (2003) Reprinted with permission from Claire R. Reeves. Claire Reeves is also the "Guardian-ad-Litem and founder of Mothers Against Sexual Abuse, (MASA). According to MASA statistics (which are probably more current than the aforementioned) "Child sexual abuse is a secret epidemic that touches the lives of far too many of our children (33% of girls and 25% of boys experience this type of abuse). Statistics like that are truly overwhelming. It is easy to feel helpless in the fight. Education is the key and one small act on your part can make a big difference."

Why Kids Don't Tell

Rarely are violence or threats ever needed to keep children from telling that someone is taking advantage of them. Innocent children, while sensing that the abuse is wrong, feel ashamed and dirty; that they are somewhat *different* than other children. A child's ability or desire to call out for help is prevented by the shame and fear they feel. It is a scary thing for a child to fear losing daddy's love or breaking up the family. They are also <u>very</u> afraid of not being believed even if they do tell. Those fears alone are enough to keep most children quiet. Abusers become quite proficient at handling these young emotions, telling the child, "Mommy may leave us forever if she finds out", or "I won't love you anymore if you tell". In my case, if you will remember, it was my Dad telling me that, "If you tell anyone, I will start with you and I will kill the whole family." That threat held me in bondage for 15 years.

But the betrayal aspect is even worse than the violation of the child's body. Our parents, aunts, uncles, grandparents or caregivers in general are supposed to be our most trusted allies. They should be our comforters, protectors, and closest friends. This is the most severe form of emotional abuse, this ultimate betrayal of our innocent trust. It's next to impossible for children to speak up against the abuse because of the loyalty and love they feel for their abuser.

Even if a child finally gets the courage to tell someone, their parents or friends many times respond to their claim with disbelief or denial. They will often judge, or even blame the child for the abuse. In my case, when I confronted my mother many years after the abuse, she suggested that it was, "Because I dressed too provocatively and just asked for it." I'm sure that at the age of three I was dressing "provocatively"; at that age I was *dressing* the way *she* dressed me. But, unfortunately, not all children find the courage or the words to let us know they are suffering at the hands of an abuser. Therefore, it has been useful to find that different organizations have come up with lists of outward signs that the child was in trouble and needed help.

Behaviors and Warning Signs of Sexual Abuse

The following is a compilation of lists of behaviors and possible warning signs of sexual abuse seen with children, adolescents, and adult women who were victims of incest and childhood sexual abuse. These behaviors may appear after a child has been known to have been sexually abused, or they may be used to identify current victims of incest and sexual abuse. These behaviors do not always mean that a child has been sexually abused, but they do mean that something traumatic has happened to the child, and we still need to see beyond the behavior to what a child is trying to tell us. Because incest and childhood sexual abuse are taboo to talk about, children often try to tell you by "acting out" behavior. Sadly, a lot of incest and childhood sexual abuse takes place before a child has words to tell you about it. I believe it is up to us as adults to look beyond the behavior and to start asking about incest, childhood sexual abuse, and other forms of family abuse. Asking a question often leads a victim to believe that you will believe and listen to the answer. Here are some outward signs compiled from a few lists:

- Unusual shyness or privacy regarding the body. Not wanting to undress in front of others at proper times may indicate feelings of an "unclean" body, or an attempt to hide telltale signs.
- Sudden, extreme changes in behavior
- Unusual interest or knowledge of sexual matters, or expressing affection in ways inappropriate for a child that age. If a child is found instructing other children in sex-related play, he may be reenacting his own real life situation.
- Nightmares, trouble sleeping, fear of the dark, or other sleeping problems
- Extreme fear of "monsters"
- Spacing out at odd times
- Loss of appetite, or trouble eating or swallowing
- Sudden mood swings: rage, fear, anger, or withdrawal

- Fear of certain people or places (e.g., a child may not want to be left alone with a baby-sitter, a friend, a relative, or some other child or adult; or a child who is usually talkative and cheery may become quiet and distant when around a certain person)

- Stomach illness all of the time with no identifiable reason

- An older child behaving like a younger child, such as bed-wetting or thumb sucking; talking baby talk

- Sexual activities with toys or other children, such as simulating sex with dolls or asking other children/siblings to behave sexually

- New words for private body parts

- Refusing to talk about a "secret" he or she has with an adult or older child

- Masturbation (sometimes very frequently)

- Talking about a new older friend

- Suddenly having money

- Wearing too many clothes

- Cutting or burning herself or himself as an adolescent

- Abuse of animals

- Cross dressing

<u>Physical Warning Signs A Child May Have Been Abused</u>

Does a child close to you or who you know have:

- Unexplained bruises, redness, or bleeding of the child's genitals, anus, or mouth?
- Pain at the genitals, anus, or mouth?
- Genital sores or milky fluids in the genital area?

Copyright Stop It Now! (2003). Reprinted with permission from Stop It Now!.

Children's Coping Mechanisms

As a way to cope with the abuse, children learn to *disconnect* themselves from painful or confusing experiences. They are able to do this by denying the experience, pretending it didn't happen to them, or by "acting it out". These "coping" methods are learned early on by victims. Some victims cope by detaching themselves mentally from their bodies. They might pretend that all fathers are sexual with their daughters (that's one of the things my Dad told me). Dad said that, "All Daddies do this for their little girls. It's to teach them how far they can go with a boy without getting pregnant." Then some victims may pretend that it is a dream, or pretend that it really doesn't hurt or bother them, or even that it is happening to someone else and not to them at all. In my own case, I didn't have to pretend. Many times when it happened to me, my body would somehow float to the top of the ceiling, and looking down, I would see it happening to another little girl. It was my "escape mechanism", and most professionals would call it "out of body experiences".

It was also amazing to me that this same father who abused me at night, could totally act the next morning as if nothing had happened. I would be forced to "keep the peace" and act "normal" and as if nothing had happened. It was just the usual morning and we were all having breakfast together. This may help you understand why the victims need to remove themselves from the abuse, or pretend. I've heard that some victims even try to inflict pain on themselves at the moment of abuse so that they can feel something else, other than the abuse. Some pretend that they are sleeping so they are not so aware of what is happening. That never worked for me; if I tried it, he would make noise and I would be afraid he would wake up the whole family. To many, it is this detachment that enables the victim to cope and to ultimately survive the abuse. Unfortunately, because of this detachment from the experience, some victims are not believed. But, whether the victim is believed or not at the time it happened, they need to know that they were not responsible for what happened; they were not to blame.

How You May Be Feeling

If you are an adult who remembers being sexually abused as a child, you may feel:

- Scared to tell anyone *"I didn't tell anyone at the time because I thought no-one would believe me."*
- Anxious and panicked (may have panic attacks)
- Sad because you lost a part of your childhood
- Guilty because you think you must have done something to make it happen *"For many years I blamed myself for the abuse because I didn't stop him."*

  Or you may feel guilty because you enjoyed some aspect as physical pleasure.
- Angry because no one protected you *"I think my mother suspected what was happening, but she was too afraid of my father to do anything about it."*
- Depressed
- Isolated
- Insecure
- Worried about what other people will think
- Confused about what really happened

If the abuser was known to you, you may also feel:

- Betrayed by him

- Ashamed at not being able to stop it

- Tricked because he called it love *"He told me he was doing it because he loved me."*

- Confused because sometimes you liked him and his interest in you

- Afraid that you've made it up

- Angry at him for what he did

  REMEMBER THIS! . . .

  - **You have a right to be angry.**

  - **It was not your fault.**

  - **You are not to blame. He was in control. He knew that what he was doing was wrong. If the abuser was somebody known to you, you trusted him. You did not make it happen!**

Copyright www.dvirc.org.au/publications/Incest.htm (2001). Reprinted with permission.

You are Not To Blame

Your life has been affected very adversely if you have suffered through sexual child abuse as I have. But, the fastest road to healing, is to place the blame where it belongs; not on yourself! You were the abused; *not* the *abuser!* The older person who betrayed you was the one who was responsible. THIS is the truth! You cannot heal and be made whole until you realize this.

We as victims have a horrible distortion of self-esteem and self-worth, and constantly struggle with false guilt, shame and secrecy. It is quite common to feel that you somehow contributed to the abuse. It certainly doesn't help to have our loved ones accuse us or tell us that we were to blame, when we were the child, and the perpetrator the adult. The encounters alone result in much confusion, guilt, shame, and outright repulsion. However, you did nothing to bring this misery upon yourself; you did nothing wrong. Get rid of any false guilt you may have! You were the child, and unfortunately, you were the victim. **You are in no way responsible!**

How The Trauma May Affect Your Life (Also quoted see below)

The trauma usually does not end when the abuse stops. Child sexual abuse can affect your life in many ways, and for many years. You may:

- Hate your body
- Not trust anyone
- Find intimacy in relationships very difficult *'I struggled with depression for years. I have only recently understood how it is connected to the abuse I suffered as a child.'*
- Feel that sex is disgusting or humiliating
- Often 'space out' and not feel present *'A big thing for me*

has been to learn to feel connected to the world again. For years I felt like a zombie, it was like I wasn't connected to my feelings or to other people.'

- Be affected physically
- Sometimes feel crazy 'without reason'
- Force yourself to be busy and 'on the move' all the time
- Feel angry at someone or angry at everyone.

Now that you are an adult you may want to look at the ways you have coped. At the time, you did not think you had many options. You did the best you could under impossible circumstances. You may have had support from someone, or you may not have told anyone.

Ideas That May Help

If you were sexually abused, these ideas may help you:

- It can sometimes help to tell another person.
- It can be a relief to accept that the abuse really happened and that it caused you great pain.
- Believe that it wasn't your fault; this lets you put the blame where it belongs, on the abuser.
- Learn to trust your memories and feelings.
- Ease the pain by crying and feeling sad
- Direct anger and rage at the abuser and those who didn't

protect you.

- Feel compassion for yourself – for the child who was frightened and powerless.

- See a counselor or join a support group.

  'Even though it may seem frightening to accept that you have been abused, it is an important step and there is support out there when you need it.'

  Remember that you have already lived through the hardest and most painful part – the abuse itself.

- You have survived.

- You can now use the strength you have gained to build a future free from the pain of sexual abuse.

- **You are not alone.** Copyright www.dvirc.org.au/publications/Incest.htm (1998-2003). Reprinted with permission.

Did You Ever Wonder: "Where Are You God?"

I guess I was very fortunate, because I always knew that God was with me. I felt ashamed at times that He must see and know what was happening to me. And sometimes I cried myself to sleep at night asking Him why He was allowing it. But throughout the Bible, He tells us that He sees everything and that He knew us before we were formed in our mother's womb. I know now that it probably greatly saddened God's heart to know that I was suffering under my Dad's abuse; seeing me endure so much pain. But I knew then and I know now that He always loved me and still loves me. He wants all of us to know Him and feel His love. But because He gave all of us the freedom of choice so that we could make our own decisions (God will never violate our will), we don't always allow God to work things out as He would like them to work out. Sometimes people just make wrong choices, like when they abuse little children. People get in the way of God's will for us.

God is not responsible for the choices of others, and neither are you. He gave us the freedom to choose. It was never in His plan for people to shut Him out of their lives and do their own thing, inflicting wicked, cruel pain on others. But He's had to watch throughout the ages while people went their own selfish way. He could stop it in a minute, ridding the earth of every cruel, selfish, abusive person. But where would that leave any of us? Most of us would have perished long before ever coming to know God's love and grace. God in his wonderful mercy gives each of us time to accept Him, hoping we won't wait too long. It says in the Bible that He has given each one of us "a measure of faith" on which to build. And further he says, "It is up to each man or woman to work out his or her own salvation." We can call on him anytime, because He's always there waiting.

Jesus longs to comfort your sorrow. He knows our hearts, and he understands what it is like for us to suffer and be treated unfairly. After all, He was sent to earth as God's only Son. He suffered and died on the cross and was raised from the dead. He did all that so that we could be forgiven. All we have to do is accept Him for who He said He was, "The Son of God." Then we can rest in a wonderfully healed relationship with Him. It's like the poem "Footprints" that tells the story of a person who doubted that God was always there, and asked, "Why Lord, when I needed you most, was there only one set of footprints in the sand?" The Lord replied, "Because it was at that moment that I carried you." I know for a fact that He carried me lovingly in His arms all throughout my childhood, and it is for that reason and more that I love Him so much today. Thank you, Lord, for carrying me to where I am today. I have such a peace and have felt your healing touch on my heart and in my mind and emotions. But, there is a key to this peace, which is also a commandment from the Lord, and that is forgiveness. Jesus said, *"For if ye forgive men their trespasses, your heavenly Father will also forgive you." (Matthew 6:14)* It is true, unforgiveness holds us in bondage and will ultimately make us ill. It is much healthier mentally, emotionally and physically to live in a state of forgiveness. I will explain more fully this element of healing in Appendix C:

Forgiveness, "Becoming God's Woman (or man)".

What If A Child Results From the Incest?

Of all the sexual taboos known to myth and anthropology, the prohibition against incest has the strongest clinical support, for the forthright reason that children born of such unions have long been known to have an unusually high rate of severe mental and physical defects. But until recently, there were few, if any, scientifically controlled studies of the children of incest. Some time ago a Czechoslovakian researcher completed such a study, and the results provided dramatic evidence that among the offspring of incestuous unions, the risk of abnormality is appalling.

Working through courts, hospitals, homes for unwed mothers and orphanages, Dr. Eva Seemanova examined and kept records of 161 children born to women who had had sexual relations with their fathers, brothers or sons. The same group of women also produced 95 children by men to whom they were not related; these half-brothers and half-sisters of the incestuous offspring formed Seemanova's control group.

The children of incestuous unions, she found, were often doomed from the start. Fifteen were stillborn or died within the first year of life; in the control group, only five children died during a comparable period. Among the children Seemanova examined at the Czechoslovakian Academy of Sciences, more than forty percent of the incest group suffered from a variety of physical and mental defects, including severe mental retardation, dwarfism, heart and brain deformities, deaf-mutism, enlargement of the colon and urinary-tract abnormalities. By contrast, Seemanova reports, none of the children born from non-incestuous unions showed any serious mental deficiencies, and only 4.5 percent had physical abnormalities. She thinks further studies of the children of incest are indicated, but believes her data confirms the "unmistakable effect of inbreeding on infant mortality, congenital malformations and intelligence levels."

Further research on my part found this article "Children of Incest" by McGillivray B. Baird PA in the National Library of Medicine Pub Med (Nov. 1982):

"Twenty-nine children of brother-sister or father-daughter matings were studied. Twenty-one were ascertained because of the history of incest, eight because of signs or symptoms in the child. In the first group of 21 children, 12 had abnormalities, which were severe in nine (43%). In one of these the disorder was autosomal recessive. All eight of the group referred with signs or symptoms had abnormalities, three from recessive disorders. The high empiric risk for severe problems in the children of such close consanguineous matings should be borne in mind, as most of these infants are relinquished for adoption."

Conclusion:

Recent research has made great strides in addressing the "what, when, where, and who" of adult-child incest. What remains almost wholly unaddressed is the mind-boggling question of "why"; something we all asked while enduring the act. First of all, incest as child abuse is not a simple phenomenon with a clear-cut pattern or dynamic. Because of its many variations, social scientists and practitioners attempting to predict, prevent, or intervene in high-risk or actual incest families find themselves confronted with a dizzying array of correlates and potential causes. Independent of this is a culturally based emotional response. The perpetration of adult-child incest is so offensive and disturbing to our everyday assumptions, that there is an immediate tendency to define such behaviors as "beyond me". In a word, it is so shocking that we literally prefer to deny that it can be understood. However, it is this author's educated and experiential understanding that it is brought on by extreme low self-esteem and probable victimization in the perpetrator's own life. They can't, or will not, deal with their own problems; don't get healing for their own abuses. As a result they become extremely controlling individuals (to finally have control over their own life), and seek out young children (often with low self-esteem) who can be easily controlled.

In 1897, near the very beginning of his psychological writings,

Sigmund Freud argued that "incest is anti-social and civilization consists of a progressive renunciation of it" (Freud, 1954). Following this lead many social theorists have offered anthropological, biological, psychological, or a sociocultural barrier. At the same time, however, the fact that incest actually occurs was long ignored or obscured. Certainly, attempts to study actual cases of incest behavior were not deemed necessary. After all, most of the traditional theories portrayed incest as virtually unheard of in civilized settings; it was assumed to be non-problematic. In that context, a social scientist who might venture to study incest cases would have run a serious risk of being viewed as a crackpot or a sensationalist, drawing attention to the exceptional rather than identifying regularities affording the basis for laws or principles of human behavior. The lingering Victorian legacy also mitigated against research on sexual topics. Thus, until very recently, academics, much like the lay public, tended to deny or evade the reality of incest, or to assume that it occurs only among the degenerate lower classes.

Following the lead of research and practice concerned with other types of child abuse and neglect, the study of incest as an actual occurrence has finally emerged as a significant research effort. A substantial body of descriptive literature is now available. It is no exaggeration to say that turning to the empirical study of incest has brought an awakening . . .finally! Long considered to be nearly unthinkable (the "great taboo"), recent findings indicate that the incestuous violation of children is one of the more frequent types of child abuse.

CHAPTER SEVEN

GROUP THERAPY EXPERIENCE

The Notice Arrives In The Mail

I held the pamphlet in my hand; after waiting for it for several weeks, it had finally arrived in the afternoon's mail. On the front cover it was entitled, "Incest: Guilt, Shame and Secrecy." Opening it, I read with anticipation as it said, "We are offering a group for incest victims which we hope will offer women an opportunity to talk more openly about their experiences in a group setting." I was already getting excited at the prospect of finally being able to share my story with others who had been through what I had. I read on, "The purpose of this group sharing is to offer group members the chance to discuss various aspects of their experience with others who can offer support, understanding and perspective. Topics which we plan to cover during the group are past and present relationships with family members, feelings about sexuality, relationships with men, thoughts and feelings about how women want their own families to be."

That sounded good to me, and I was already sure that I wanted to be a part of this group. But, first, I wanted to ask my friend, Dana Gamble, to attend with me. She and I had shared our experiences over the past couple years, and I really felt that she might gain a lot from it, too. Actually, another reason I was asking her was that I really needed the moral support. After all, I was going into unfamiliar territory, and even though I was excited about sharing my story, I was also nervous about it. So I called Dana and read the pamphlet to her over the phone. After reading her the part I have already mentioned above, she listened as I read the rest of the pamphlet.

"For many women, the worst part of being an incest victim is the damage done to her self-esteem and the negative feelings about herself which linger long after the actual incest is over." We both knew that and had shared with each other how it had negatively affected our lives. I read on, "Because incest victims rarely talk about their experiences with others who have had similar experiences, they often feel isolated and ashamed." We could both agree on that! It went on to say, "It is hoped that the personal sharing and group interaction will help break the barrier of shame and silence that so frequently occurs with incest. We will also provide time for each woman to assess her current needs and to make plans for any future counseling or other intervention once the group has ended." It continued with the date, time and place of the meetings, mentioning that they would hold four meetings on Thursday evenings following one day long meeting; sessions would be about an hour and a half.

Then it mentioned "<u>Group Expectations</u>": "In addition to the expectation that group members will hold all material shared in the group confidential, there are two additional expectations: 1) that each group member will be willing to talk about her incest experience with the group, and 2) that each member agrees to come to a total of five group sessions."

Then at the end of the brochure it said, "<u>Nitty Gritty</u>": "A screening interview with one of the group leaders must occur before a group member can be accepted into the group. Payment will be based on our sliding fee schedule. More information about the group can be obtained by calling either of the group leaders at . . ."

When I got to the end of the brochure, Dana was as excited as I was, and we decided to call them right away. We were able to set up a screening interview for us the following week. Because we lived over 50 miles from where the meetings were to be held, Dana and I decided to always drive into town together. We kept our appointment, and following our discussions with the counselor, it was determined that we both would profit from what the group could offer. We were both excited as we were accepted, and looked forward to the meetings as if they were a new adventure. It certainly would prove to be.

The First Session:

The first meeting, which was the daylong meeting rolled around before we knew it. After getting my daughter set up at Dana's house to baby-sit her son, we headed into town; both of us with great expectations, but a little reservation. We had no idea what the evening would hold for us or for the others we would meet at the meeting. But, as we arrived, we could see the same expressions of wondering on the other young women's faces. We were all venturing into unknown territory. The counselor came into the room, introduced herself, and asked that we move our chairs into a big circle so that we could begin to share. Then, when all was arranged, she had us go around the circle, each one stating our names and where we were from. That didn't take very long; there were just fifteen of us in the group, but representative of many personal stories, as we would soon discover.

As each young woman shared her story, we were aghast to learn how many of us had suffered similar, but sometimes very different, kinds of sexual child abuse (incest). Most of the time the girls cried as they told their stories, but we all listened, because it was our story, too. We could very much relate to their pain and suffering, to their heart's cry at the indignities and betrayals they had all experienced   It was so hard to admit what had happened.

While I was telling my story, it seemed as if it were yesterday, and it all came to the surface, all the old feelings that had been shoved down deep into my soul for so long. I couldn't hold back the tears any more than any of the others; it was hard to get through the story while this overwhelming grief poured out of me. When I composed myself, I finally struggled through to the end, and sighed with relief. As we finished our day, the counselor told us that we had made a lot of progress; that we had really gotten through the most difficult part, and that in the meetings to follow, we were going to concentrate on healing and getting better. That was encouraging, but I can't tell you how tired we were after the meeting. We felt completely drained and exhausted; it had been so emotional to "get it all out". Dana and I discussed it on the way home, and were both comforted knowing that we could share our feelings with a good friend who understood. The ride home passed very quickly and we were home.

The Second Session:

Then a week passed and it was time for our first Thursday evening meeting. Again we drove into town as we discussed how we'd been feeling throughout the week. It had been good, and we were beginning to think that maybe there was some light at the end of the tunnel. Time would tell. When we got to the meeting, the counselor was again putting our chairs in a big circle, but with one difference. This time there was a <u>huge</u> pillow out in the center of the room. We all wondered what the pillow was doing in the middle of the room. We would soon find out. When we were all seated, the counselor told us that we were going to go around the circle, and each of us would share how we felt toward our abuser. We were to each of us in turn, go out to the pillow and, pretending that it was the abuser, do anything to it that we wanted. We could kick it, hit it, spit on it; do whatever came to mind. A lot of the girls after expressing how they felt toward their abuser, went out and got their exercise, so to speak. They whaled on that thing!! Some girls viciously kicked it, some got down on the floor and just beat the thing to death, and yes, a few spit on it and voraciously directed their opinions at it. It was liberating for all of them; you could tell; you could see it on their faces, the sense of triumph over their abuser.

Dana and I had been sitting together, and they had started with her, so I was the last one to share. When I told them how I felt toward my Dad, and all the deep resentments had been expressed, I just broke down and cried; I couldn't even move, and remained seated instead of venturing toward the pillow. The counselor said, "Sandy, out of all the girls, you have probably endured the longest and most violent abuse of anyone here; WHY can't you go out and do anything to the pillow?" I sat very still, trying to think of why I wasn't moving forwarding, showing my frustrations and retaliating against that pillow. I couldn't stop crying, but I knew I had to answer her. I opened my mouth and practically yelled, "Because I don't have a butcher knife!" Wow! I didn't know until that moment how much I really hated him, and how much help I really needed. I had actually come into this group with the idea of getting more feedback from other people for a book I had promised to write someday. When I was a little girl, I had written the poem that appears in the front of this book, "Father, Forgive My Father", promising God that someday "I'd write a book, and make others take a look". Little did I know that I had so much hurt, frustration, and downright hate locked up inside me, that I wanted to *kill* my father?

Walking Through Steps Toward Healing

As a result of this revelation, during the course of the group counseling sessions, the counselor suggested that I confront him, telling him how I deeply resented what he did to me and ask for an apology. Even then, at that age (my early 30s) I reasoned that I could not do that; I knew it would send him into a crazy rage, that it would endanger the family. There was still so little that law enforcement or other agencies would do in those days; and, obviously, he still held me in bondage at that point in my life. So, I just continued to keep an eye on him and tolerate him. But down deep, he must have known what he was missing. Because I didn't trust him to be alone with my daughter, he lost out on the experience of being a real grandpa; and all of our children missed out, too. But I did go through the steps to forgive him (mentally, verbally, and emotionally) because I knew what the Bible said about forgiveness: "For if you forgive men for their transgressions, your heavenly Father will also forgive you. But if you do not forgive men, then your Father will not forgive your transgressions." (Matthew 6:14-15) I truly hope and pray that my father on earth asked forgiveness from our Father in Heaven before his life was over. He was given every opportunity when finally our confrontation came, but as you will probably remember from a previous chapter, he only said, "Well, Dear, I will just say that I am sorry for anything you *think* I did. But, sometimes you have a vivid imagination." So, he was still in complete denial, and I never did see any remorse or get the apology I so desperately needed. I asked him again, much later on, if he was all right with the Lord, if he knew he was going to heaven when it was his time. He said, "I've asked the Lord to forgive my sins, and I think that's all that's necessary." He wasn't about to ask for my forgiveness, or that of anyone else in our family, even then. If he had truly been repentant of his sins, he would have found it necessary and been more than willing to ask forgiveness of those he had hurt. Unfortunately, we saw no evidence of remorse in him ever.

Therapy sessions with abusers reveal that if a sexual

offender shows no remorse, he probably is capable of repeating the offense, and many are repeaters. I should have reported him for that reason alone, but instead we all just kept our eyes open, watching his every move and not letting him be around our children or other small children. We reasoned then that that was enough, but it wasn't. Abusers should be reported, no question about it, and made to answer and pay for their sins, and then to get help and counseling to recover from their abusive past.

As Claire R. Reeves stated in her book, "The secrecy and shame associated with incest families too often rally around the perpetrator instead of comforting the victim. Perpetrators never have just one victim. Unhealed survivors of the same perpetrator must find the courage to protect other youngsters in their family; not heap more abuse on the whistleblower."

Bringing it into the light can be a life-saving measure. Leaving it in the dark can be a destroyer. But unveiling the pain means letting the light shine on all casualties: the innocent target, the perpetrator, and other family members. Therapists agree that the earlier incest is confronted the sooner healing can begin. Forgiveness may not occur, nor may there be reconciliation, but patients can start over. Claire Reeves went on to say, "Healing and moving on is the best revenge, and talking about it is still the best way to start that healing process. The younger any survivor can begin dealing with the abuse he or she suffered, the longer he will have to lead a full, happy life. Healing may be a lifetime journey, but it does not have to be all sadness and trauma."

For one woman (among many) the specter of incest has arrived in her golden years. She is not the injured party; she is the one caught in the middle. She can't stand seeing another article or talk show segment on the subject. She is the mother of an incest victim, married to the perpetrator for 52 years. He is now disabled and legally blind, and their daughter, the accuser, is in her 50s. "I'd like to close my eyes and never open them again." She said, tears welling in her eyes. "I'm angry and I'm hurt."

The truth may reveal why the daughter has suffered a lifetime of dysfunctional behavior – an inability to keep a job or maintain a secure relationship, a pattern of abusing drugs and alcohol. "But why", the mother asks, "must this all come out now?" This mother could not understand, why, when they had been so generous to the girl and given her everything (like cars and houses) that she could ever need or want, was she about to sue them for $275,000 in emotional damages. Because of the new statute of limitations laws in most states now, there are many victims who are finally suing their abusers for atrocities that happened many years ago, but have affected them all their lives.

"It is not easy for older generations to peel away the layers of a less than perfect life. They are the ones who were told to pick themselves up by the bootstraps, to face life like John Wayne, to quit being a sob sister," said the developmental director at Central Washington Comprehensive Mental Health. "On the other hand, we think it is important to confront perpetrators. We don't think it should be ignored," he said. "If there is one lesson that comes out of their experience it is the value of intervening early so they can resolve it and it doesn't come to this."

The sensationalism of celebrity incest victims coming forward may wear off, but the problem must be acknowledged. I'm sure you've seen it, too; it's on "Dr. Phil", it's on "Geraldo", and on the "Montel Williams Show". Maria Shriver and Oprah have interviewed women victims, and Roseanne Arnold and Oprah have both declared themselves survivors. The specter is incest. Its victims know no age limit, cultural, social, economic or educational defense. It is the severest degree of the child abuse tragedy. We acknowledge it and we think it is an important topic. But, like it or not, it's a part of the community and we have to deal with it.

It is rare for people to take civil action against their parents, but as more cases come to light it is becoming more common. Monetary awards might have a way of redressing a wrong these people feel has been done toward them. Whether or not such action results in healing can be debated. Money will not salve or "heal" the pain a victim experiences. For me it would not be healing or rewarding. Understanding the trauma is a key to recovery, but not *the* key to recovery. It is **forgiveness** (of which I will expand on in Appendix C). Forgiveness may not necessarily occur, but individuals must somehow bring closure to the incident so it no longer haunts their lives.

For the family we've spoken of in this chapter, the wounds are only now being opened, the pain only now unveiled – when all are nearing old age. Whether justice will be served and healing achieved is questionable. What is clear is that all suffer when it comes to the hidden sins of a family. For this family, the solution may not lie in financial security for one at the expense of financial ruin for elderly parents. There have been enough victims; there has been enough pain. But there is much need for counseling. Therapy is needed to heal the wounds of a family who possibly has been out of control for many generations. It is a well known fact among therapists that mothers and fathers in these families may have come from dysfunctional family systems themselves in which they were not safe. Incestuous fathers and boyfriends were often victims of sexual or physical abuse by their own parents. Many times the abused *become* the abuser. Mothers who keep the incest secret are likely to have been victims of physical or sexual abuse as children. They are most often described by others as passive, withdrawn, and extremely dependent. When confronted with the horror of sexual crime in her own family, these mothers are prone to use the psychological defense of "denial". I know my mother did, and still does to a certain extent. She has said that she is sorry and that she has deep regrets over letting it happen, and I know that she is sorry. We have shared our feelings, and I have forgiven her. She, too, was held in bondage by my father.

It is likely that the child will feel betrayed by her mother, who did not provide protection. The victim is also likely to have mixed feelings toward an abusing father; the father may be seen not only as exploitive, but also as the child's only source of affection. Treatment of the dysfunctional family system is necessary in most cases.

Adult survivors of incest often seek individual therapy (or group therapy as we did) at some point in their lives to counter their self-depreciating beliefs and to deal with the ghosts of the past. A study of women who sought therapy for the effects of incest revealed these characteristics of their past abuse:

- Trouble developing intimate relationships with members of either sex.
- Wanting to become less trusting (they already reported low levels of trust)
- Unassertiveness and self-abasement
- Feelings of worthlessness and helplessness

- Lack of enjoyment of sex

- Involvement with men they perceive to be like their fathers, that is cold, domineering, self-centered, exploitive.

- Significant discrepancies in their self-images, feeling they are very different from the way they would like to be (very lacking in self confidence)

- Very prone to eating disorders

While the actual incidence of incest is unknown, the sexual abuse of female children is estimated to range around 600,000 cases a year. Some researchers believe the number of cases is underestimated because many victims' stories are disbelieved and go unreported. Even therapists have been known to be skeptical that incest occurred. Freud even doubted his patients' reports of incest, partly because he found it hard to believe that actions like that against children could be so widespread. Victims experience further trauma when they find the courage to seek help and their reports of incest are not believed. It is better to have faith in the child's reported abuse, and get them the help through counseling that they need; sooner, rather than later, as was stated earlier. It is also *very* important to provide strong reassurance that it is not her fault since, in fact, a child cannot seduce an adult. It is very helpful to the child's psychological wellness if parents indicate that they are responsible for the child's lack of safety. This relieves the child of the guilt and shame she has thrust upon herself, and begins her road to recovery.

In summing up this chapter, I would say that the group therapy experience was very helpful to me and I gained a lot. I learned that I was not alone in my suffering, that others had been going through similar abuses, and that we were all in a healing process. It was refreshing to share with others who understood and could relate to us. It completely broke the long bondage of *secrecy*, and it was like a huge weight had been lifted off of us. So for me, it totally removed the aspects of guilt, shame and secrecy. However, I found that that wasn't enough; I needed to walk through the steps of forgiveness to be totally set free. Unforgiveness in our lives can actually lead to illness, and no one wants to be burdened with that for the rest of their lives. As a result, I went through those steps, and during my years of living in Alaska, went a step further and put together a workshop called "Becoming God's Woman (or man)". The workshop teaches the steps to total forgiveness of those who have hurt you, so that you're able to be a useful individual in our society. So that you can be the healed and whole person that God *wants* you to be and *meant* you to be. After all, God is in the business of restoration.

Restoration

Many people enjoy restoring objects from days gone by. Whether it is an old automobile or boat brought back to life (as my husband loves to do in his retirement), a radio that now works again, or furniture that shines once more, it is a feeling of accomplishment to see the old made new. God also does restoration. We know many people who need their lives restored (healed). God can take a life that is broken in pieces and put it back together in a way that makes it better than before. But He will not do so unless we ask Him. He will not force his will upon us. But when we ask Him, He will answer and begin to reveal himself in deeper ways. Jeremiah 33:3 tells us: *"Call unto me, and I will answer thee, and show thee great and mighty things, which though knowest not."* God wants to heal you of those hurts of the past. Why not give Him a chance? Good advice comes to us through this passage in the Bible:

"BUT THOSE WHO WAIT ON THE

LORD SHALL RENEW THEIR STRENGTH.

THEY SHALL MOUNT UP ON WINGS AS EAGLES,

THEY SHALL RUN AND NOT BE WEARY,

THEY SHALL WALK AND NOT FAINT."

ISAIAH 40:31

Walk through the steps of forgiveness in the back of this book, asking the Lord to help you to have a forgiving heart. That first step is so important. However, don't forget that most of us need to talk with a professional and get some good counseling from people trained to help us, whether it be individual or group therapy. Then, REMEMBER: reach the point where you have what I call "tough love" with yourself. Ask yourself, "Just how long am I going to let this thing (these hurts of the past) affect my life?" Reach a determination that you are NOT going to let it affect you hereafter. You have to come to that realization that to ask for forgiveness and to ask for God's help is not going to do it if YOU keep taking it back from Him, savoring the hurt and mulling it over and over. You've all seen these people who just refuse to get on with life, and have constant pity parties, blaming everyone else for their life failures. Well, I refused, and that is what YOU need to do. This example of moving on was clearly demonstrated by the apostle Paul in his Epistle to the Philippians: *"Brethren, I count not myself to have apprehended: but this one thing I do, forgetting those things which are behind, and reaching forth unto those things which are before, I press toward the mark for the prize of the high calling of God in Christ Jesus."* Philippians 3: 13-14

CHAPTER EIGHT

PROFILE OF AN ABUSER

Again, who ARE these abusers? As was stated earlier in this book, they are people we usually know; 90% of child abuse is by someone the child knows such as a neighbor, family friend, babysitter, grandfather or grandmother, uncle or father. Fathers, about one-half biological fathers and one-half stepfathers, represent the most common offenders. However, child molesters defy the stereotypes we have created. It would be easy if we could look at a child molester and identify him or her by physical or behavioral traits. Unfortunately, this is not possible. There are a number of common myths about individuals who abuse children:

Myth No. 1: The child abuser is a dirty old man.

Myth No. 2: The child abuser is a stranger.

Myth No. 3: The child abuser is retarded.

Myth No. 4: The child abuser is alcoholic or drug-addicted.

Myth No. 5: The child abuser is sexually frustrated.

Myth No. 6: The child abuser is insane.

Myth No. 7: Child abusers progress over time to increasingly violent acts.

Myth No. 8: Children are at greater risk of sexual victimization from "Gay" (Homosexual) adults than from "straight" (heterosexual) adults.

Myth No. 9: Child abusers look "icky" or unkempt.

By realizing that these are myths, we should understand that child abusers have the same general characteristics as the rest of the population, and it is not an easy task to identify the individuals who constitute a risk to our children. It is interesting to note, however, that often our children have a sixth sense about individuals who may hurt them; so it is prudent to be aware of this and listen to our children when they feel uncomfortable around someone.

There is no clear cut profile of a sexual offender, or of how someone becomes one, however, research has shown that child abusers come from all walks of life; from all ethnic and economic groups. Most abusers are not criminal or anti-social in other parts of their lives. Many have good steady jobs, support their families well and are active in the church or community. This you will remember was the case with my father, who was a professional person in a scientific field, and a leader and teacher in the membership of a local church. They seem generally to be liked by others, but have few close friends. Most are socially inadequate and form few close relationships. Often they are bossy and controlling and like to dominate their wives and children. Although on the outside they appear normal, they frequently feel ashamed or bad about themselves.

They seem to cover up insecurity and dependence by acting 'macho' or domineering. The sexual abuser is exceedingly self-centered and meets his/her own needs often at the expense of others. Probably half of the offenders begin to have deviant fantasies or begin the pattern of sexual offense in their teenage years. About 90% of all abusers were molested as children themselves or saw this as a model (for example, father molesting sisters).

The sexual offender goes through certain psychological processes which allow him to commit the sexual offense. Through what is known as cognitive dissonance he does something even though he knows it is morally wrong and illegal. Cognitive dissonance is a process in which a person justifies his/her behavior by changing the meaning of it, e.g., "I'm just doing it for sex education." If you will remember, that is the reasoning my own father used: to teach me how far I could go with a boy. In addition to this rationalization (excuse making) there are often environmental circumstances which contribute to the onset of the problem, although these don't need to be present for the abuse to continue. The abuser uses some method of getting the child to cooperate: physical force, intimidation, threat of getting in trouble, bribery, or just doing it. Abusers also try to keep the abuse a secret by not physically hurting the child and by making sure the child won't tell. This is usually done by making the child feel it will be his or her fault if anything bad results from telling anyone.

There may be related problems in the marriage if the offender is married. In some cases, physical violence, most often directed toward the wife, is present. The offender frequently disapproves of family members' involvement in outside activities and tries to limit their contacts. He seems jealous, suspicious and almost paranoid about others. He usually blames others for anything that goes wrong, rarely acknowledging his own responsibility in a situation. This often leads to disturbed family relationships, with confusion related to parent/child and brother/sister roles.

The offender does not consider the child's feelings when he abuses her. While few offenders recognize the psychological impact of what they are doing to the child, many do feel badly afterwards. An example of those feelings is evident from these words from a recovering offender: "I have only recently begun breaking down walls and layers of defenses, seeing myself for who I am and empathizing for all those I have hurt. Get to me with your messages before I reach my trigger—those feelings of fear and paranoia and feeling desperately and utterly alone." Copyright Stop It Now!. (2003) Reprinted with permission from Stop It Now!. www. stopitnow.org

Stop It Now! Is speaking to the need of abusers who cry out for help. Their "daring innovation is to create a forum in which the survivors of child sexual abuse, their families, and recovering sex offenders can step forward, "speak up", and work together to end the cycle of abuse. We have collected demographic and lifestyle information about abusers from survivors and have encouraged recovering sex offenders to write publicly about their commitment to stop the abuse now." Copyright Stop It Now! (2003) Reprinted with permission from Stop It Now!. www.stopitnow.org.

We could hope that most abusers, after reading these words, would want to step forward and get help so that they could stop it now:

"You have no idea how much of an impact your actions have on a child,

how it can absolutely devastate a person's life, and how much work it takes

to reverse the damage done. You must realize that no matter how small you

consider the act you have done, it has changed that child and will have

lasting consequences. I can only hope and pray that you get help so you will

not repeat the offense. It is up to you to stop the cycle now."

--Words of a survivor speaking to abusers

"Will Abusers Respond To Our Call To STOP?

Before the Stop It Now! Helpline, some abusers called authorities and turned themselves in. Abusers in prison tell us that they wish there had been a helpline for them. We know there are abusers who understand what they are doing is wrong; these abusers are the most likely to call for help." Copyright Stop It Now! (2003). Reprinted with permission from Stop It Now!.

If you or someone you know needs this kind of help, please call the helpline below:

Stop It Now! 351 Pleasant Street, Suite B319, Northampton, MA
01060
Helpline: 1-888-PREVENT (1-888-773-8368)
Tel: (413) 587-3500 Fax: (413) 587-3505
E-mail: info@stopitnow.org

Another thing you can do, to be absolutely educated and be better prepared to protect your children from sexual abuse in your area, is to contact the web sites of these two very good resources:

The National Alert Registry

(It costs just $10 for a full report: Neighborhood Predator Report)

at www.nationalalertregistry.com

and the FREE listing on-line by states at www.prevent-abuse-now.com

EPILOGUE: By Forrest Don Lee

As of this time, Sandy and I have been together for six years and married for four. At the time we met, she was in the process of getting her Dad away from her Mother, and into a care facility for those suffering from dementia. Had I known the extent of her Dad's abuse to her, I would not have been able to be civil to him. Perhaps it's best that I didn't know.

By completion of this book, Sandy has fulfilled a life long dream to tell her story and how, through the Lord's help, she was able to survive life and eventually forgive her father. Her desire to help other victims to heal has truly been guided by God's helping hand.

In the past little was known about the extent to which abuse of this nature affects the victim's whole life. However, now we know that the affects reach far beyond the actual act into adult life, and even sometimes long after the perpetrator is deceased.

Although our life has been enriched by our companionship and true love for each other, it is my feeling that the ugly affects of the abuse she suffered still linger, and in some ways to this day, affect our married life and intimacy. But we know, that as a happily married couple, we must work daily to overcome these adversities in "Becoming God's Woman and Man"…of "excellence" (the best that we can be).

APPENDIX A

THE SIGNS THAT SPELL ABUSE:

"Most of us teach our children to be polite to adults, and it is important to have nice manners. However, you need to teach your children that not all adults are nice people. If an adult makes them feel "icky" or "uncomfortable", they need to tell you." Claire R. Reeves, "Childhood-It Should Not Hurt".

But what if they *don't* tell you? We as parents, or concerned adults, need to know the warning signs that could spell abuse. In my search for information I found many good lists that can be helpful in recognizing that a victim is in need of help. At first I wanted to combine these lists, but for the sake of giving credit where credit is due, I will list them separately, according to publication or author.

SIGNS & SYMPTOMS: Claire Reeves, author "Childhood-It Should Not Hurt" Mothers Against Sexual Abuse, (MASA).

- Sexually acting out with other children
- Excessive masturbation
- Night Terrors (nightmares)
- Fear of bathrooms
- Fear of adults
- Constant vaginal infections

- Blood in underwear or diaper

- Age inappropriate sexual knowledge

- Use of vibrator or other sexual paraphernalia

<u>Child Sexual Abuse Includes Touching and Non-Touching Behaviors</u>: Copyright Stop It Now! (2003). Reprinted with permission from Stop It Now!. <u>www.stopitnow.org</u>.

Touching behaviors include:

- Touching a child's genitals (penis, testicles, vulva, breasts, or anus) for sexual pleasure or other unnecessary reason.

- Making a child touch someone else's genitals, or playing sexual ("pants-down") games.

- Putting objects or body parts (like fingers, tongue or a penis) inside the vulva or vagina, in the mouth, or in the anus of a child for sexual pleasure or other unnecessary reason.

Non-touching behaviors include:

- Showing pornography to a child

- Exposing a person's genitals to a child

- Photographing a child in sexual poses

- Encouraging a child to watch or hear sexual acts either in person or on a video

- Watching a child undress or use the bathroom, often without the child's knowledge (known as voyeurism or being a

"Peeping Tom").

If you have any questions about these or other signs and symptoms, please call the Stop It Now! Toll-Free Helpline at 1-888-PREVENT.

Behavioral Warning Signs A Child May Have Been Abused:

Some of these behavioral signs can show up at other stressful times in child's life such as divorce, the death of a family member, friend or pet, or when there are problems in school, as well as when abuse in involved. Any one sign doesn't mean the child was abused, but several of them mean that you should begin asking questions. Do you notice some of the following behaviors in children you know well?

- Nightmares, trouble sleeping, fear of the dark, or other sleeping problems
- Extreme fear of "monsters"
- Spacing out at odd times
- Loss of appetite, or trouble eating or swallowing
- Sudden mood swings: rage, fear, anger, or withdrawal
- Fear of certain people or places (e.g., a child may not want to be left alone with a baby-sitter, a friend, a relative, or some other child or adult; or a child who is usually talkative and

cheery may become quiet and distant when around a certain person).

- Stomach illness all of the time with no identifiable reason
- An older child behaving like a younger child, such as bed-wetting or thumb sucking
- Sexual activities with toys or other children, such as simulating sex with dolls or asking other children/siblings to behave sexually
- New words for private body parts
- Refusing to talk about a "secret" he/she has with an adult or older child
- Talking about a new older friend
- Suddenly having money
- Cutting or burning herself or himself as an adolescent.

Copyright Stop It Now! (2003). Reprinted with permission from Stop It Now!. www.stopitnow.org.

Physical Warning Signs A Child May Have Been Abused:

Does a child close to you have:

- Unexplained bruises, redness, or bleeding of the child's genitals, anus, or mouth?
- Pain at the genitals, anus, or mouth?
- Genital sores or milky fluids in the genital area?

If you said "yes" to any of these examples bring your child to a doctor. Your doctor can help you understand what may be happening and test for sexually transmitted diseases.

Have you ever seen someone playing with a child and felt uncomfortable with it? Maybe you thought, "I'm just over-reacting", or, "He/She doesn't really mean that." Don't ignore the behavior; learn how to ask more questions about what you have seen. For a more complete list on warning signs to watch for, please call the Stop It Now! Toll-Free Helpline at 1-888-PREVENT. Copyright Stop It Now! (2003). Reprinted with permission from Stop It Now!.

As I stated before, there are many good sources out there (especially on-line today) to locate lists of warning signs. I was able to find a few more general warning signs in miscellaneous news publications. Some behavioral signs are likely to appear over a longer period of time and later on be more noticeable. Specific behaviors indicating the possibility of sexual abuse are:

- Reluctance to be left alone with a particular person
- Prostitution
- Wearing lots of clothing; especially to bed
- Drawings of genitals
- Fear of touch
- Abuse of animals
- Masturbation in public

- Apprehension when subject of sexual abuse is brought up
- Cross dressing
- Loss of appetite
- Irritability, crankiness, short-tempered behavior
- Needing more reassurance than usual, clinging to parent
- Changes in behavior at school or in relating to friends

No single indicator is proof that a child is being abused. It is, however, a reason to look more closely at the child's behavior and to consider the possibility of abuse. We do, however, need to be watchful when dealing with young people, and IF they do finally confide in you, BELIEVE them. The child's emotional health may be determined by the reaction of the parents (or other care giving adults). In order to resolve the emotional trauma and return the child to normal functioning, the parents *must* believe the child and never blame the child. Most children when finally coming forward are telling the truth; it is rare that they are not. The parents will need to alleviate their personal distress without further exacerbating the situation. Read further in Appendix B for agencies you may contact for helping the victim.

APPENDIX B

The sexually abused child is not only a victim of sexual exploitation, but of societal attitudes which tend to disbelieve or blame the child. She or he may be traumatized by the sexual abuse and be additionally traumatized by the reactions of those she turns to for help. It is imperative that the goal of intervention be to focus on the needs of the child by protecting her from further abuse and minimizing the emotional trauma.

What To Do Immediately

1. Go with the child to a private place. Ask the child to tell you what happened in her/his own words, and listen carefully.

2. Tell her/him that she/he did well to tell you, that you are very sorry this happened, and that you will protect her/him from further molestation.

3. If you suspect your child has an injury, contact your regular physician or a local medical center's emergency room immediately.

4. You may call the police immediately and a uniformed officer will come to your house to take an initial report.

5. You may call your local Sexual Assault Center and ask for an emergency room social worker for advice and information about what to do.

No matter how well you think you know your children, you may never know what they're hiding inside. Children who have been sexually exploited are usually at a loss for words; silence speaks to the fact that less than 35% of these victims report to the police. So keep a careful eye on your children. Make them feel comfortable and safe enough to tell you any problems that they may be having. To report child sexual exploitation, call the police. Then call the National Center for Missing & Exploited Children at 1-800-843-5678 or contact them at www.cybertipline.com

This organization works tirelessly with law enforcement to bring these child molesters to justice. Just as important, they give victims a voice, so that an unspeakable act never leaves a child speechless for life.

There are many such groups of which I have compiled the list that follows:

- Mothers Against Sexual Abuse (MASA), P. O. Box 371, Huntersville, NC 28070. Or contact at www.againstsexualabuse.org

- Stop It Now! 351 Pleasant St., Suite B-319, Northhampton, MA 01060

  Or contact at www.stopitnow.org

- Kids Helping Kids at www.kidshelpingkids.net

- VOICES in Action, Inc. (Victims of Incest Can Emerge

Survivors

P. O. Box 14, Newtonsville, OH 45158 or call 1-800-7-VOICE-8

www.voices-action.org

- Pittsburgh Action Against Rape (PAAR), 81 South 19th Street

  Pittsburgh, PA 15203-1852 or call 1-866-END RAPE

  (24-Hour Free & Confidential Hotline)

- Family Resources (Preventing Child Abuse by Strengthening Families), 141 South Highland Avenue, 2nd & 3rd Floors, Pittsburgh, PA 15206 or call 412-363-1702

- Witness Justice, P. O. Box 475, Frederick, MD 21705-0475 Or call 301-898-1009 or email info@witnessjustice.org

On May 4, 2005, I was privileged to listen to a broadcast of World Talk Radio. The program Darkness to Light: "Breaking the Conspiracy of Silence" featured Claire Reeves whom I have mentioned many times in this book. She emphasized that to prevent our children from being victimized, "we *must* educate ourselves and our children; education is POWER." She went on to say, "Educate your child as young as two years old; teach them their body is their own and to not let anyone touch them *where a bathing suit covers.*" I believe that is a good guideline and one that any child can understand.

Reeves also cautioned that if your child has been abused by a spouse or other family member, "Do not take the child and run and hide. Then the courts have found the *real culprit* and you will be up for kidnapping charges." This just makes a bad situation so much worse. It is far better to report it and get the victim educated help and counseling.

More ways in which you can help following the assault are:

1. Continue to believe your child and do not blame your child for what happened.

2. Consult with your physician or the Sexual Assault Center regarding need for medical examination.

3. Instruct your child to tell you immediately if the offender attempts sexual molestation again or bothers her/him in any way.

4. Give your child reassurance and support that she/he is okay and safe.

5. Respond to questions or feelings your child expresses about the molestation with a calm, matter-of-fact attitude, but do not pressure your child to talk about it.

6. Respect privacy of the child by not telling a lot of people or letting other people question her/him.

7. Try to follow regular routine around the home (expect usual chores, bedtimes, rules) to have continuity of 'normalcy'.

8. Inform brothers/sisters that something has happened to the child, but that she/he is safe now and will be okay. Do not discuss details of assault with the child's siblings. Make sure that all children in the family are given enough information to protect themselves from the assailant.

9. Take the time to talk over your feelings privately with someone you trust: your spouse, a friend, a relative, a counselor; express your feelings. Do not discuss situation repeatedly in front of your child/children

A few other people to contact for help or counsel are listed below:

- Child Protective Services
- Local Divisions of Family & Youth Services
- Church (your pastor or priest)
- School Counselor or Favorite Teacher
- Crisis Intervention Services

[What is most important for you as someone who cares about the child is to say that no matter what happened or what they say, you will still love them. Also take the time to reassure the child that he or she has done nothing wrong. Let the child know that you will do whatever you can to keep him or her safe. Many people are tempted to handle the disclosure on their own. However, there are resources throughout the country that can help a family through this difficult situation. Furthermore, the sexual abuse of children is against the law. It is, therefore, important to seek professional help and to not do this alone. By taking action you may reduce the risk of others in your community or family from being sexually abused.] Copyright Stop It Now! (2005). Reprinted with permission from Stop It Now!. www.stopitnow.org

APPENDIX C

"BECOMING GOD'S WOMAN (OR MAN)" of
Excellence
(God's Woman/Man of *Excellence* = God's *Character)*
Psalm 27:1)

Workshop Outline

Did you know that the only people who are really free are the ones who walk in a spirit of forgiveness? Then we should all begin to forgive and quit harboring unforgiveness in our hearts. Did you know that unforgiveness actually causes harm to our body, emotions and mind? But, you know: sometimes the human being just enjoys self-pity and recognition for being mistreated. The longer you're on that little pity party and the more they say to console you, the better you like it; so you let Satan feed your flesh. But this way of thinking and behaving can be costly, and if we are to be honest with ourselves, retaliation and revenge are just not worth it. Most abuse cannot be repaid; you can never say enough or pay back enough for what they did to you. An unforgiving spirit can rob you of what God has for you, and you are being unforgiving to someone the Lord has already forgiven. It is much easier to stand the pressure of forgiveness than the incarcerated bondage of unforgiveness.

My Testimony

This book is my testimony, however, my life as a wife, mother of two and grandmother of 14, and the healing I have experienced are further testimony to God's loving guidance throughout my life. It has been a very eventful life, filled with early betrayal and rejection by an abusive father resulting in loss of self- esteem and three failed marriages. But God was in the midst of it all; never failing me, and showing me unconditional love and acceptance. Life for me began again when I was forty years old when I started over after losing my home, husband and children, all within the year of 1983. It began a time of healing and facing up to everything in my life up to that point. It took me a long time to come into "Becoming God's Woman" and I'm still working on the "excellence" part. I think that is going to be a lifelong process, because I always want to be open to what God wants to teach me. This workshop centers on what the Holy Spirit and experience have impressed on me as being most important in starting the healing process. I'm so thankful that I can share it with you.

Outline:

I. Be Healed In Jesus Name: Is. 42:9

    A. Emotional Wounds - Is. 43: 18-19

    1. Child Abuse - Job 11:16

2. Divorce - Is. 48:6

3. Abortion - II Cor. 5:17

4. Alcohol/Drug Dependency - Is. 65: 16-17

5. Strongholds - II Cor. 10: 3-5

Examples of needing healing:

- Bitterness & Resentment

- Compulsive Behavior

- Depression

- Defense Mechanisms

- Rebellion

- Violence

- Suppression and Denial

Can you think of others?

Decision: You have to make a conscious decision to have *Tough Love* with yourself – ASK: Just how long am I going to permit this thing to hold me back from ALL that God has for me? Then make a decision to forgive and accept healing in Jesus' name. (Phil 3: 13-14)

B. Physical Infirmities

1. Already done - (OT) Is. 53:5(NT) I Peter 2:24

2. All Diseases - Psalm 103:3

3. All People - Luke 6: 19

C. In God's Time

    1.   Immediate - Luke 8:47 } Testimony of both healings

    2.   Over time period

    3.   Everywhere – no geographical or physical boundaries He is everywhere waiting to heal us.

II. Forgive - NOTE: Again, the only people who are really free are the ones who walk in a continual spirit of forgiveness: The Word commands us to forgive. Matt. 6:14-15, II Cor. 2:10-11, I John 1:9, Col. 2:13 Ourselves, too! Psalm 79:9

  A. Unforgiveness - Mark 11:26

    1.   Can cause harm to the body, emotions & mind; thus, hinder Christian growth.

       a.   Health Problems=

       b.   Mental Problems=Many months/years of

       c.   Emotional Problems=counseling & therapy

    2.   Costly

       a.   Retaliation = lost energy to "get even"

       b.   Vengeance = lost sleep/time (insomnia) – preoccupation with wanting to hurt back

       c.   Family and loved ones suffer neglect.

B. Six "R"s of Forgiveness:

1. **Repent** of attitude – ask God to change your heart toward that person.

2. **Release** them emotionally; must give it to God completely.

3. **Recognize** them as a tool in the hand of God to free you of your own unforgiveness.

4. **Remember** God's grace and how many times he's forgiven you.

5. **Reconciliation** – confront the person to get it right!

6. **Rely** on the Lord to give you the strength and words to do it. - Eph. 4:32

NOTE: If they are deceased and you cannot personally do this, mentally set them in a chair and tell them of your unforgiveness; then tell them you forgive them.

C. Why Don't We Forgive?

1. Procrastination – we keep putting it off for one reason or another.

2. Fear – mostly of the reaction or consequences (the unknown)

3. Sometimes the human flesh enjoys self pitty and attention

for being mistreated. Remember....we're letting Satan feed on us.

D. Evidence of Forgiveness

    1. Feelings against them no longer there. You can see them, but you're FREE!! Gal. 5:1

    2. You can accept the other person for the way he/she is.

    3. When your concern is greater for that person than the wrong they did you. You want to minister to them and help them. The whole tone of the relationship changes! P.T.L.!!

III. Love - Lev. 19:18

A. Unconditionally as He has loved us.- Eph. 3:14-19

B. All peoples (our neighbor) - Matt. 22:39, I Pet. 4:8

C. Family and Friends - John 15:13

D. The Unlovable (our enemies) - Matt. 5:44, I John 2:9

IV. Have Busy Hands/Purpose - Psalm 90:17

NOTE: Happiness has been explained by some as having:

    -Someone to love

    -Something to do, and

    -Something to look forward to

<u>Therefore, it is most important to have goals.</u>

V. Have Goals Read Prov. 31:10-31 as a personal devotional

As you read, look especially for this woman's character qualities. See how many of the following qualities you can find: surrender, obedience, discipline, purity, discretion, gentle and quiet spirit, and wisdom. This completeness of character and grace could only flow from vital godliness. The priority in this woman's life is seen in verse 30 – her **fear of God.** It is her spiritual life that is commended and is foundational to her "excellence".

VI. Exercise

A. Our body is the temple of the Holy Spirit: John 2:19-21, I Cor. 6:19

B. Strenuous exercise burns off excess hormones that can cause us anxiety and add to monthly symptoms.

C. You'll have more energy and feel sense of well-being.

D. You'll be more attractive and desirable to your husband.

VII.Have a Heart for God's Word (Main FOCUS)

Scripture memory enables us to keep our goals in mind and open our hearts to the transforming work of the Holy Spirit. Romans 12:2 David wrote, "I delight to do Thy will, Oh my

God; thy law is within my heart." (Psalm 40:8) Having God's Word in our hearts is great motivation to obey and to grow. God calls us as men and women to "excellence"—it is not *perfection,* but essentially a desire to be strong in and for the Lord, and the best that we can be. Can we all so appreciate the marvelous salvation of Jesus Christ that we are our utmost for His highest?

Closing: Early in my life I responded to God's love for me. Knowing that God loves me unconditionally has freed me from trying to live the Christian life by being perfect; trying to *earn* His love by performing. My understanding of God's constancy in His love encourages me to return His love by living a life that brings honor to Him. I want to become "God's Woman" (a woman of excellence); not because I have to perform, but because I choose to please God! Praise His Holy Name!

BIBLIOGRAPHY

Olson, Doris Green Fisher. (Reprinted 2004). *Another Tomorrow.* Bloomington, IN: Author House.

Reeves, Claire R. (2003). *Childhood, It Should Not Hurt!.* LTI Publishing, Inc.

U.S. Department of Health and Human Services, Administration on Children, Youth and Families, *Child Maltreatment 2000.* (Washington, DC: U.S. Government Printing Office, 2002).

Berliner, L., "Child Sexual Abuse: What Happens Next?". Victimology: An International Journal 2:327-331, Summer 1977. "Children of Incest, 1972). Newsweek (Science Section).

"The Montel Williams Show". CBS. February 2, 2004.

Foltz, Linda Lee. (2002-2003). *Kids Helping Kids Break the Silence of Sexual Abuse.* www.kidshelpingkids.net

"Darkness to Light: Breaking the Conspiracy of Silence". World Talk Radio. May 4, 2005.

"The Sound A Child Makes When Sexually Assaulted Is Often Silence". (2004, January). *Better Homes & Gardens, Monthly Magazine.*

The Domestic Violence and Incest Resource Centre (1998-2003)

publications on-line.

Victoria, Australia. www.dvirc.org.au

Stop It Now!. (2003) publications on-line @ www.stopitnow.org

POEM: "The Magic of Love", Helen Steiner Rice. Used with permission of The Helen Steiner Rice ™ Foundation, Cincinnati, Ohio www.helensteinerrice.com. Copyright 1970 the Helen Steiner Rice ™ Foundation – All Rights Reserved.

ABOUT THE AUTHOR

The child had a vision: "How do I help other kids get through this pain?" During years of reconstructing her fragmented heart, she knew her commission: fulfill her childhood promise to God. SANDY LEE was a leader of Cub Scouts, 4-H, and church youth groups. She studied under the Sitka Christian Counselors Association, and presents a workshop entitled "Becoming God's Woman/Man". Retired in 1998, she and her husband reside in Washington State. It is her hope that this book will be instrumental in helping to heal hurting young people and adults. She wants to see people set free from the bondage of sexual child abuse and bring them the peace that only God's healing touch can give.

FOR ORDERING COPIES OF THIS BOOK

PLEASE CONTACT WEBSITES BELOW

Printed in the United States
38407LVS00006B/220-363

9 781420 866506